Wolverine

SIERRA TRAIL RUNS

A GUIDE TO THE EASTSIDE

Dan Patitucci, Janine Patitucci,
Hjördis Rickert, & Kim Strom

Wolverine

SIERRA TRAIL RUNS: A GUIDE TO THE EASTSIDE
Authors: Dan Patitucci, Janine Patitucci, Hjördis Rickert, and Kim Strom
Design: Wolverine Publishing, LLC, and McKenzie Long at Cardinal Innovative
Maps: The authors and Wolverine Publishing
Photos: PatitucciPhoto
Artwork: Ann Piersall Logan
Published and distributed by Wolverine Publishing, LLC.
© 2022 Wolverine Publishing, LLC.
International Standard Book Number:
978-1-938393-45-7

Printed in South Korea

For more info, visit **sierratrailruns.com**
Follow @sierratrailruns

ANN PIERSALL LOGAN
Ann is the artist behind the artwork featured in this book and AnnieP Fine Art and Darn Fine
Hats. She lives in Bishop, California, on the east side of the beautiful Sierra Nevada. Ann's art
is inspired by the colors, geometry, and adventures in the places she loves. **annieplogan.com**

DISCLAIMER

This book is not a definitive or exclusive source of information. Self-reliance is key. Anyone
undertaking the runs detailed in this book is solely responsible for their own safety. They
should use good mountain judgment, complete thorough route research, be physically and
mentally prepared and properly equipped for the challenges, and should be ready to turn
back if conditions become more demanding than their abilities can handle. The authors and
publisher accept no responsibility for injury, damage, or loss to body, possessions, or vehicle
as a result of using this book.

long may you run

Imagine this
Big mountains
Desert Below
Snow
Sun
All together as One

It's a beautiful day
Sun is gettin' low
Time to take a stroll
Grab the wheel and drive slow
In this land I call home
Eyes fill with desert snow
Sagebrush aroma seepin' into my nose
At the same time, spirits wakin' my soul
I see how far I've come
And how far I've got to go
Yet this moment right here
Gonna go with it and flow
Like the water as it winds
From the mountains to the valley
Let the bad thoughts pass
And go right out me
Catch the good ones
Hold 'em like my greatest dreams
Keep my eyes open
Watch my life like a screen
But this ain't no drama
No I'm livin' a love song
Rightin' my wrongs
And lovin' every step I stand on
Catchin' myself when my mind gets weak
Expecting excellence every time I start to speak
What more can you ask when this life is a gift
I chose to be here
So I live it up to the fullest

Live It Up *Lyrics by Kwa-Z*

CONTENTS

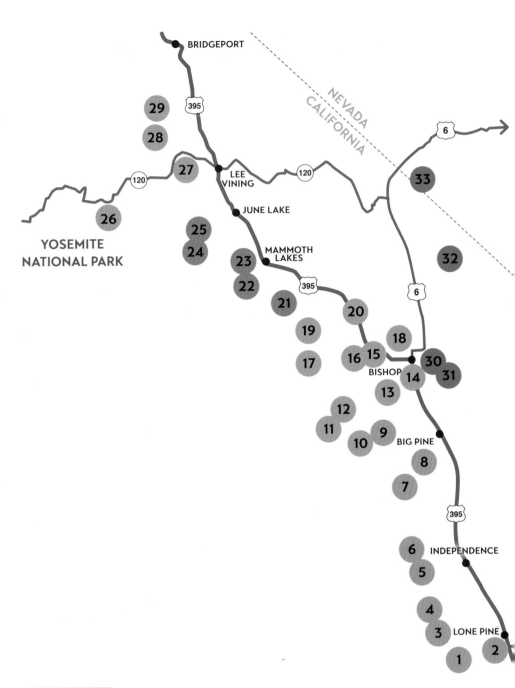

GPX TRACKS

OVERVIEW OF RUNS

95

BEATTY

374

95

DEATH VALLEY
NATIONAL PARK

36

136

190

35

190

34

DEATH VALLEY
JUNCTION

178

127

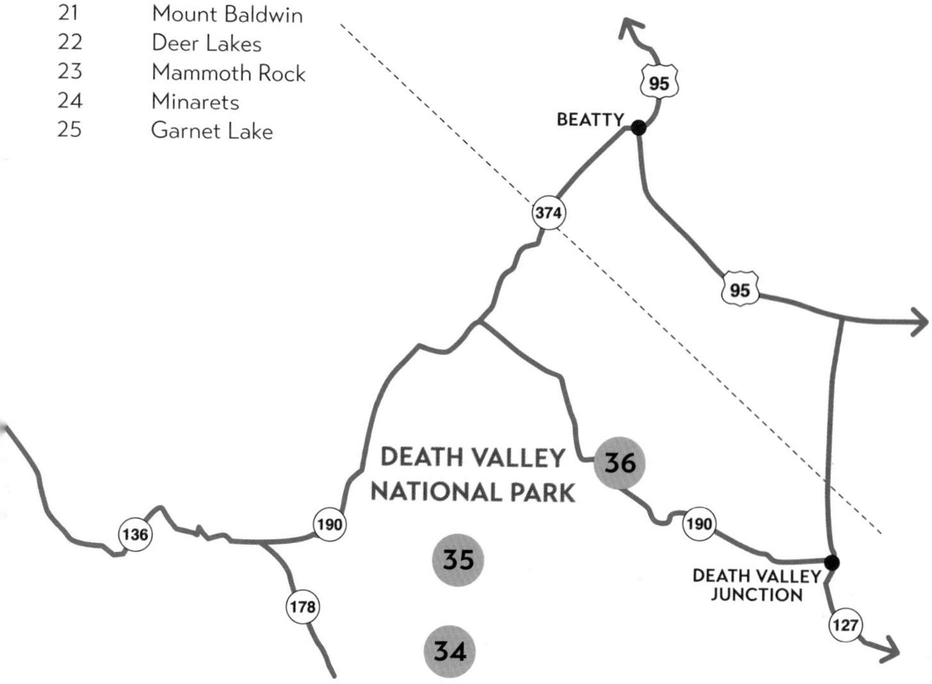

COMMON GROUND

Dan Patitucci

"Sir, the John Muir Trail is not a day hike."

For the Wilderness Permit Officer, dealing with overly enthusiastic under-prepared day hikers was business as usual. My friend, John, was ready to launch an unassisted attempt at the Muir Trail's FKT (Fastest Known Time). Trying to insert the square peg of trail running tactics into the round hole of mainstream mountain travel, John Stamstad, owner of numerous ultra-endurance titles, awkwardly stammered his response: "For me it is."

The square peg grated the lip of the round hole.

"And where will you camp?" He looked up from his fingernails to assess this character.

"I won't."

"But you have to sleep."

"I'll only nap during the day."

"How will you store your food?"

"I'm not camping."

On it went, until with a supervisor's approval and a sworn statement that he wouldn't camp or even nod off at night, we left the building, permit in hand.

About 100 miles into John's run, I rejoined him on Muir Pass. He had yet to sleep and his hand bottles had frozen during the night. We shuffled along together through the Evolution Basin, John nodding hellos at trailside boulders he mistook for hikers.

John's day was simple: keep moving, keep eating, and stay out of trouble. As trail runners, we each do this when we set out for a day in the mountains. Simplify the process so we can maximize the experience. Leaving behind what we *think* we need, we can benefit from the things we *do* need. Pre-dawn, headlamp-illuminated dust, a glowing pink sunrise sweeping over granite, growing warmth to the heat of mid-day, chickadees calling out their cheeseburger song to those who'll listen. We run through sage and boulders beneath a vast blue sky, breathing air thin with elevation. All reversed as the sun drops with the scent of the land shedding the day's heat. Despite his stumbling, John wasn't suffering at all.

That was in 2005, when you had about as much chance of tipping back a frothy IPA in Bishop as spotting a trail runner in the backcountry. Nowadays, there isn't such a collision of mentalities, and there are plenty of local brewery options. Trail running has grown from a training activity for climbers, hikers, skiers, and even road runners into a sport and culture all its own.

In typical California fashion, Sierra trail running combines a certain level of peak performance and dirtbaggery that breeds legends from ordinary outliers and tumbleweeds capable of extraordinary toughness. It's an ideal setting for pointless but essential human tricks; accumulating two million vertical feet of gain in a year, running a car-to-car of Mount Whitney in roughly three hours, or establishing the Goliath Traverse, an astounding 32-mile technical ridge link-up of the Sierra crest in an incredibly fast and impossibly long eight days.

In a region full of guidebooks, this is the first trail running guide to the Eastside. A responsibility comes with that: to encourage this attitude of athleticism, resilience, discipline, curiosity, quirk, and self-reliance. And to educate runners to move respectfully through a landscape that does not belong to us, with as little impact as possible.

When it was time for me to leave John, I watched him shuffle away in his floppy hat to face his second cold night out. Standing there in the silence, I came to understand all that is possible in the Sierra Nevada. A witness to beauty, inspired by potential, I turned to face my direction and started on my own way.

OUR HOME: SINCE THE BEGINNING OF TIME

Kris Hohag

Equipped with a pen, gifted with a voice, Kris Hohag, aka Kwa-Z, is an artist, father, and educator in the Eastern Sierra. A citizen of the Bishop Paiute tribe, and a descendant of the Mono Lake Kutzadika Paiute Tribe, he founded Legendary Skies Enterprises, LLC, to offer local indigenous cultural ecotourism and promote tribal business leadership. Legendary Skies Enterprises works to promote wellness, prosperity and sustainability for all indigenous communities, with a particular focus on youth.
More info: legendaryskiesenterprises.com

*Disclaimer: This essay is NOT a comprehensive history of Nuumu people everywhere, nor all native people here in Payahuunadu. I share these words with a good heart and intentions, and I hope this reaches those who care and will benefit. And most importantly, that we all do our part to protect this place.

This chapter is intended to be more than a mere "Land Acknowledgment." Such requests have been catching on over the past few years, and if not given proper consideration, they can come off as very performative and shallow, if not offensive. This is giving (some) voice to the (many) silent stories that have existed here since time immemorial. The intent in putting these words down is to encourage you to learn more and perceive this place in a new light.

Over the past 150 years, what little has been written about this place has mostly come from white males, with a few rather powerful female authors lending their voices as well. With the exception of Sarah Winnemucca Hopkins and Viola Martinez, most accounts have been from the settler view. But Indigenous authors? Not so much. This land has thousands upon thousands of years of history that predate the classic American narrative that we have grown up hearing and likely passing down ourselves. This place has so much more to it than that.

Stories upon stories, originated from generations past too long ago to remember exactly when. From the People that have lived and thrived here, at times just barely survived; yet enough for one generation to tell them to the next. We are fortunate to have some of these stories still here. Our language survives, and we are working to bring it back to good health and value in our communities. Our songs and dances are getting stronger, and the old ones exist with the new. Our communities are scattered but tight knit.

The Founding Fathers of the United States understood this was Indian land. They said as much in their own words. They claimed it anyway. This land is where cultures collided, power and politics divided, trauma was induced and healing continues. The story of America is the story of Native American homelands being turned into American real estate in the form of either private or public lands. Land stained by our ancestors' blood. Water runoff and aquifers tapped by the City of Los Angeles for the past 100 years have depleted, but not killed our spirits. This place is so very much alive despite the colonial human impact.

With that classic wild west, manifest destiny context set, you cannot stereotype this place. It is one-of-a-kind in my experience. This land is very special. You, insightful reader, may know this. Perhaps that's why you are reading about it. But perhaps you are a trail runner from some distant place who just happened to stumble upon this book and are thinking of coming here. Or perhaps the echoes of your homies raving has put the Eastern Sierras on your bucket list, for good reason.

Part Great Basin, part Sierra Nevada. Part desert. Part mountains. All natural abundance. A place renowned for its majestic natural beauty, powerful earth energies and ample silence to meditate on the things that really matter. The open space to see and seek for miles and miles and quiet space to clearly hear the Creator speak.

Our people have known and respected the sacredness of this place for millennia. Not only that, but indigenous peoples from all over Turtle Island likely have come here to receive its medicine, long before capitalism became the dominant cultural institution. Humans have had thousands of years of lived experience in this land. The origin stories of Nuumu ("Numa") or Paiute people

are rooted among this landscape. We call the area "Payahuunadu" or "the place where the water always flows" because that has been the experience for the native people living here. Life is dictated by the water flows and seasonal cycles.

I think about how and why I chose to participate in this book. Love of this place. Love of our people. Taking up space. Taking care of each other. Respect. Faith in humanity, and our resilience to heal and help others. I am an advocate for health and wellness, Tribal sovereignty and I am a proud protector of our homelands. If being involved in this book can help more native people or anyone in my family begin to run these trails that our people used for millennia, then I will have succeeded. Many of the trails in use today are old Indian trails that evolved into trails for public use. When we get on the land, we reconnect with the footsteps of our ancestors. Here in the Sierra Nevada, it is very literal, as the landscape hasn't changed all that much in the mountains since colonial contact. Over thousands of years, our elders tell us there is hardly a place a Native has not set foot on this land.

Alongside our ancient legends and traditions, we have tragedy of the likes we are still recovering from. In 1863, our native people were forcibly marched at gunpoint out of this land and many were lost in the process. Some escaped into the mountains for their protection, and others survived the march all the way to a distant prison camp. Eventually, many of them too returned to their beloved homelands, while others married into other nearby tribes. Attempts to erase our existence and narratives have not prevailed and we must never stop telling our stories as indigenous people.

In these times of climate catastrophes, political and economic instability and social upheaval, it is important to respect the indigenous perspectives of these lands. Lands upon which many people now call home and claim to love, but far too few

truly know about the history of how things came to be. For too long native ways of thought have been suppressed, buried, even outlawed. Yet here we are. Still living between the mountain peaks and walking the trails of our ancestors. Still continuing our ways. Still resisting colonialism. We are a part of this land. I feel it in my bones and my flesh. As my grandparents came and went, I too will one day return to this earth. I feel good to know I come from this place and I care for it as I care for my own family.

When it comes to running or even just being out on the land, I feel my modern life day-to-day worries dissolve as I sync into the higher vibrations that come with being among the mountains, under the great blue sky, sun on my skin. Leaving the man-made society under artificial light for a few hours or days and being in the dwelling place of the Great Mysterious Creator — I feel better just thinking about it.

For many, running is more than a recreation or exercise. It is a means to getting somewhere. It is the vehicle by which we travel, and at one time, we all traveled by foot. Our traditional societies had runners to take news to other neighboring camps. We traded and made relatives with tribes across the Sierra. In that way, it is a primal thread that runs through all cultures and lineages. Human beings are walking, talking, running (when not driving) mammals.

When I run on the track or the long flat paved road, the ground is artificial and hard. The redundancy of the environment lulls my attention and my stamina is limited. When I run on the land, my spirit runs free. My mind leaves and thoughts fly away, not hindering me. I feel the air and smell the plants. The path winds and dips, then climbs and turns. Maybe I just wanna jump over a rock or juke out a bush. I can have fun with it. **Running through the landscape on trails and animal paths, we become one with nature again.**

TYPICAL GUIDEBOOK STUFF

The Sierra Nevada mountain range in California spans approximately 400 miles from the Mojave Desert in the south to the Cascade Range in the north, and averages 70 miles in width east to west. The vastness and diversity of the range encompasses terrain through an array of climate zones, hundreds of peaks, passes, and deeply carved watersheds. It is home to 26 wilderness areas, three distinct national parks, and two national monuments. Much of the Sierra and surroundings to the east are protected, to varying degrees, by the designations of Wilderness, National Forest, National Park, and Bureau of Land Management public land.

The Eastern Sierra is characterized by a steep escarpment with nearly 11,000 feet of abrupt relief from the valley floor to the highest peaks of the crest. Known as the "Range of Light," the High Sierra is predominantly composed of light-colored granitic rock and washed in morning alpenglow and abundant daily sun. It is remarkably bright and open, owing to its glacially carved expanses dotted with sparkling lakes and sparse trees.

East of the Sierra and bound on its opposite side by the Inyo and White Mountains is the Owens Valley, the deepest valley in America at 25 miles wide and over 10,000 feet deep. The Owens Valley might easily be glossed over as barren high desert, but the magic of this land and its cultural history, flora, and fauna are as much a treasure to the Eastside as the mountains it lies between.

The eastern Sierra and Owens Valley, along with the White and Inyo Mountains, Panamint Mountains, and Death Valley, are part of the Great Basin, a large geographic feature inside which the watersheds are landlocked. They also make up the western reaches of an expansive zone known as the Basin and Range Province, which extends east across Nevada into Utah and far south into Mexico.

ACCESS

The Eastern Sierra is remote and distances can be far between locations. The nearest larger airports are in Los Angeles, Reno, and Las Vegas. Small airports in Bishop and Mammoth have limited commercial connections to bigger hubs.

GEOLOGY

The Sierra Nevada are predominantly granitic in composition with some metamorphosed remnants of pre-existing rock and sediments. Millions of years ago, these rocks were formed and cooled deep beneath the surface during the zone's chapter of subduction. While the mountains of that time have long since been eroded, subsequent uplifting, westward tilting, and erosion have exposed the granitic batholith, carved by episodes of Pleistocene glaciation into the spires, cirques, and wide valleys that they are today.

Geologically recent and ongoing volcanic activity is evidenced by frequent earthquakes, cinder cones, lava flows, geothermal hot springs and venting. One of the world's largest calderas, the Long Valley Caldera, outside Mammoth, and surrounding landforms consisting of welded ash, pyroclastic flows, and obsidian domes are all examples of this activity.

CLIMATE

The Owens Valley has a climate of extremes. It's hot in summer and cold in winter: average highs at the peak of summer are near 100 degrees Fahrenheit, while winter daytime highs hover in the mid-50s and overnight temperatures dip into the low 20s and colder. The High Sierra, however, is typically mild in summer, making it comfortable while the valley is roasting (as long as you avoid mosquito blooms).

Characteristically, the region has long shoulder seasons that offer some of the best use days. Heavy on sunshine and predominantly dry, the Sierra and surroundings offer weather conducive to running year-round either in the mountains, on the flanks, or on the valley floor,

especially when compared to most other mountain regions. Summertime can develop thunderstorms and occasional monsoonal patterns. Winter brings variable dry periods interspersed with storms. In big snow years, the Sierra Nevada, meaning "snowy mountain range" in Spanish, is known to accumulate 8-foot dumps in a single storm.

With the effects of climate change blatantly evident in prolonged drought cycles, late summer and fall also face the challenges of a long, dry fire season.

HISTORY

A few brief paragraphs cannot begin to do justice to the area's multifaceted, complex history. This book includes indigenous names of peaks and places when known, in the hope that they become reestablished and more widely used as the common names. The land these trails run through has been home for millennia to the Nuumu and Newe, Timbisha, and Kawaiisu people, and their ancestors before them. The Nuumu call this valley Payahuunadu, the Land of Flowing Water. Their connection to the valleys and mountains wells from thousands of years of life deeply interwoven with the waters and a stewardship of the plants, animals, and land they hold sacred.

What followed, when settlers discovered the area's prospects for mining and ranching, was a tragic and brutal period that resulted in loss of life and land to the native peoples. Mining ran the course of its inherent booms and busts and is still a source of poignant pressure on sacred lands today. The Los Angeles Department of Water and Power (LADWP) stands prominently with its own sordid role in steering the pathways of modern history and the current status of land ownership and water rights. While the LADWP is responsible for diversion of the eastern Sierra waters, its actions have resulted in a limit to development and expansion in the Owens Valley.

Below are some good resources to begin learning about the area's past, the importance of honoring the native peoples, and supporting land-conservation efforts into the future.

Bishop Paiute Tribe and Youth Council
bishoppaiutetribe.com
Friends of the Inyo
friendsoftheinyo.org
Eastern Sierra Interpretive Association
sierraforever.org
Eastern Sierra Land Trust
eslt.org
Eastern California Museum
inyocounty.us/ecmsite
Laws Railroad Museum
lawsmuseum.org
Owens Valley Indian Water Commission
oviwc.org
Walking Water
walking-water.org

HIGH SIERRA & THE EASTSIDE

The runs in this book are all accessible from the east side of the Sierra Nevada mountain range. Listed generally from south to north, these routes span the area between Lone Pine and Bridgeport along Highway 395, then further east to the White Mountains and Death Valley.

BETWEEN THE PINES

The zone between the towns of Lone Pine and Big Pine is the true High Sierra, where trails tend to be rocky, have huge relief, and reach high elevation. The highest point in the Lower 48 is here, and many of the runs have the biggest gains per go. Trails in this region are rugged, tough, alpine, and accessed from an area with limited services.

BISHOP

This is the hub of the Sierra Eastside. Bishop's central location makes it a great place to base for reaching most of the range. Here the rugged High Sierra begins its taper, providing access to higher-elevation runs that escape hot desert summers and to lower-elevation trails for year-round running. The biggest town on the Eastside, Bishop has full resources, micro-breweries, running shops, and world-famous climbing and bouldering.

MAMMOTH

The Mammoth area is best known as a skiing and mountain-biking destination. Its summits are a little lower, and the terrain offers softer, friendlier, and more worn trails with plenty of shade. Colder winters and milder summers have trade-off benefits for year-round running.

TUOLUMNE AND NORTH

Tuolumne Meadows is the eastern gateway of Yosemite National Park. It's a must-see destination for its famous domes and grassy meadows. North of the Meadows, the peaks and passes become smaller and lower approaching Bridgeport. With the less dramatic landscape come fewer crowds.

WHITE MOUNTAINS

The White and Inyo mountain ranges parallel the Sierra on the eastern side of the Owens Valley. They are stark, barren, and dry. The ancient bristlecone pines grow here where little else survives. Runs through this wild and raw landscape typically include brutal vertical gain and reach high elevations. Lacking the sharp spires of the Sierra, the Whites and Inyos seem less imposing, but wandering their trails reveals just how massive they actually are.

DEATH VALLEY

Death Valley is a great place to avoid in the summer. This national park brags record high temperatures and the lowest elevation in the country. Running through this inhospitable but gorgeous landscape is better done in winter, although some higher areas in the park can be surprisingly cold.

WHERE THE MOUNTAINS MEET THE SKY

BROKEN ARROW SKYRACE

OLYMPIC VALLEY

PRESENTED BY
salomon

LAKE TAHOE

52K • 26K • 11K • VK • TRIPLE CROWN
IRON FACE CHALLENGE • KIDS RACE

BROKENARROWSKYRACE.COM

BEFORE YOU GO

This book is a starting point. It'll get you to the trailhead with a plan. The routes and photos are meant to inspire and provide information, but you'll also need an understanding of the current conditions, an accurate map, experience, and some stamina.

THE LEGWORK

TRACKS

In the spirit of fast-and-light, you're not going to run with this book tucked into your vest along with the crumpled wind shell, soft flasks, and empty bar wrappers. The written route descriptions will get you through the basics, but you'll want more detail on the trail. Downloadable GPX tracks are available at sierratrailruns.com on the GPX TRACKS page. Use the password: **eastside**

MAPS

Maps are critical. Most runs have connecting trails that can complicate navigation, but are also useful to make the routes longer when

you're not ready to be done, or shorter in case of uncooperative weather, injury, or if you run out of steam. Save a photo or print of the run map for while you're out, and keep the track available for offline use in your preferred mapping app. Gaia, FATMAP, and CalTopo are a few recommendations.

SEASON

In a typical year, most runs in the High Sierra are doable from mid-June to mid-October. This is dependent on the amount of snowfall from the previous winter and the aspect of the slopes. Many of the EASY runs and lower-elevation trails are accessible year-round. These are typically best done outside

the hottest months. If you do run in hot landscapes during summer, go early in the morning to avoid extreme heat.

ROAD CLOSURES
Many mountain roads and passes are closed during winter months, approximately November to May. Always check for road conditions and closures to be sure you can get to where you're going: roads.dot.ca.gov

SNOW
Before you go, consider the aspect and elevation of your run. Trails on north-facing slopes can hold snow late into the summer. Take poles or microspikes if you think they might be useful.

ALTITUDE
Many of these runs go high, or even start high and stay high, for long stretches. For most people, acclimating is key for health, a successful day out, and is a responsibility to running partners. Understand how your body responds to higher elevation and prepare accordingly. Typical altitude issues include headaches, nausea, fatigue, malaise, lack of appetite, and the general inability to get out of first gear. Read up on preparing for high altitude starting on page 34.

WATER
Carry a sufficient amount of water and be prepared to spend more time on the trail than you think. It's possible to get water from streams and lakes on many of the runs. Filtering or purifying is necessary. There are, however, routes with no access to water. Particularly in the White Mountains, there may not be water for long stretches or at all. Leave yourself a jug to chug from when you return to the trailhead. You might look forward to hydrating even more than eating a burrito.

APPROACH
The Sierra is rugged, and not just for running. Trailheads can also be difficult to get to and from. Access varies. Some of the more frequented trailheads are reached by paved

roads all the way to paved parking lots. Others require high clearance or 4WD to maneuver over dirt roads to a turnout in the sage. The drivability of dirt roads can change season to season. Driving tips are included in each run's APPROACH as needed.

STATS

All distances and elevation gains are approximated based on our watch recordings combined with figures from various mapping platforms. Cross-country routes have the added complication of wandering. Everyone may travel a different line, adding a variable that can, over longer runs, add up to very different distances. When you're ready to be finished with a run, it's usually best to assume there's more left than you think. Always pack some extra calories.

TRAIL BETA

These are some tips to help you navigate or prepare for each route. TRAIL BETA gives you a little extra turn-by-turn when there's a turn you definitely don't want to miss.

A LITTLE SOMETHING EXTRA

Some favorite side trails and detours are recommended as A LITTLE SOMETHING EXTRA. If you've got time and extra energy for another summit or nearby swim, try these.

PERMITS

We all like spontaneity and free access to mountains. Not many runs in this book require a permit or a fee, but routes that do are noted. Runs inside national parks require an entry fee, and if you want to split a longer run into a two-day fastpack, you'll need a permit for backcountry overnights. For permits visit: **recreation.gov**

COMMUNICATION

Let someone know where you are going and when you expect to return. Phones are unreliable at best in the front country and don't work at all in most of the Sierra backcountry. If something happens, you are likely facing a long haul before reaching assistance.

EMERGENCY

Anyone undertaking these routes should be self-reliant. Accidents can happen in the mountains where it is difficult to reach assistance in an emergency. A satellite communication device (SAT) may be useful, or if you are in range of cell service contact: 911.

ADDITIONAL RESOURCES
More info, more resources, more knowledge.

Sierra Trail Runs	sierratrailruns.com
AirNow	airnow.gov
Inyo County	inyocountyvisitor.com
Bishop	bishopvisitor.com
Fires	inciweb.nwcg.gov
Inyo Info	fs.usda.gov/inyo
Leave No Trace	lnt.org
Lone Pine	lonepinechamber.org
Mammoth	visitmammoth.com
National Park Service (NPS)	nps.gov
Permits	recreation.gov
Road Closures	roads.dot.ca.gov
Weather	noaa.gov/weather

SAGE TO SUMMIT

Inspiring mountain athletes since 2006

ON THE RUN

TRAIL-RUNNING GEAR LIST

What you carry depends on the season, conditions, your personal experience and preferences. Take enough to be safe, but not too much to prevent moving efficiently. It's crucial to find the balance between under-prepared and over-burdened. A few suggestions of what to bring:

Running pack
Weather-appropriate clothing
Rain or wind shell
Gloves
Hat, buff
Sunglasses
Sunscreen / mosquito repellent
Headlamp
Soft flasks or water bladder
Water purification
Nutrition and hydration
Waste and WAG bag
First aid kit
Phone or sat device

Additionally, poles and gaiters are useful on many of the bigger mountain runs.

Poles: Lightweight running poles can be a huge advantage on long climbs. They can also add extra stability for creek crossings, snowfields, and may prevent an ankle roll.

Gaiters: While not at all necessary, gaiters can keep you from feeling like you need to stop and dump piles of decomposed granite (DG) and prickly things out of your shoes every few steps. Leave the trail on the trail and save your feet from abuse. Gaiters are especially useful for traveling through scree.

SELF-RELIANCE

The Sierra range is massive and wild, and the nearest water or town can be a long way away. There's no shortage of objective hazards like exposure, remoteness, weather, and rockfall. Conditions up high and on north-facing trails can be very different than in the high desert valleys. Know your abilities and limits as you'll need to be physically and mentally prepared for long days in changing mountain conditions. Take along good judgment, and avoid needing rescues that have additional impacts in the wilderness. For either a self-rescue or activated emergency response,

the seriousness of even a minor injury, like a rolled ankle, can have major implications for all involved. Plan to be self-reliant in the event that something does happen; assistance is a long way off.

TRAIL ETIQUETTE
"LEAVE NO TRACE"

Never before have there been so many user groups visiting the Owens Valley and Eastern Sierra. This is the first guide to trail running in the region, which carries a tremendous responsibility to encourage an ethic of leaving the places we run better than we find them. Respect for the local residents, history, traditions, environment, and other visitors is critical to sustain everyone's access to nature and recreation.

BE PREPARED

Prepare for your wilderness experience without counting on external support while on the trail. Prior to any activity, a run, a hike or even a visit to a new area, consider thorough research. Study your maps for available water sources, terrain features, and bailouts to avoid any surprises while on the go. Weather should be taken seriously, so even though it's sunny California, check the local forecast. Always be prepared with proper gear and an understanding of the environment you'll be passing through. Stashing supplies to support any backcountry recreational activity is illegal and inappropriate. Your responsibility is not just for yourself, but for the others in your group, and for any emergency crew that would have to be activated in case of a rescue.

PACK IT OUT

Beyond egg shells, banana peels, and wrappers, one of the biggest topics is, of course, pooping. No matter how good your Leave No Trace skills are, pooping is the one aspect of your impact that you might be able to significantly improve. Many of us have been taught to dig a cat hole 6-8" deep and fill'er up, or to use the smear technique and let the sun do its work. In the high-desert environment, however, these are not the best strategies. Dry ground and insufficient composting bacteria may not break down what you've deposited. It'll live on for animals to get into or pollute nearby water sources.

NEVER leave toilet paper behind. This goes for number ones, too. Nix the toilet paper and use a soft flask for a trail bidet. When you do use paper, pack it out in a dedicated ziploc.

The best method is to use facilities whenever available. When that's not possible, simply pack out your own poop in a WAG bag. Mountain shops offer a surprising number of options these days in the pooping aisle. Dog-mess bags work just as well. Nothing says respect for the environment like a warm bag of poop in your running vest.

This goes for all waste, even waste that isn't your own. Pack out anything you take in and if you see garbage that someone else has left behind, pack that out too. Help leave a place better than you found it.

LOW IMPACT

All zones in the Eastern Sierra and high-desert environments are very slow to recover from human imprint. From car tires to campsites, and even foot traffic, any tread you leave behind will be around for quite some time.

Minimizing impact also extends to leaving what you find. If everyone takes something, soon there will be nothing left. Leave rocks, plants, archaeological artifacts, and other objects as you find them for whoever comes after and for the animals that rely on this environment for their food and shelter.

FIRE

Much of the Eastern Sierra is dry and extremely prone to fire. This is a huge problem for the region, and wildfires are often caused by human negligence. For cooking, use a camp stove responsibly and don't start a fire.

WILDLIFE

The wilderness these trails travel through is home to many species of animals. Don't disrupt their habitat and keep them wild by not feeding or approaching them. For their protection as well as your own, avoid bears, rattlesnakes, and mountain lions, all prevalent in the Sierra down to the lowlands. If you do encounter a bear or mountain lion, don't try to outrun it. They are faster trail runners. Instead, back away slowly, make noise, and try to make yourself look as large as possible.

Bear boxes are provided at many of the trailheads. Always leave your food, anything that smells like food, and containers that might hold food in the provided bear boxes. Leave nothing in your car that might interest a bear.

SHARE THE TRAIL

Many of these runs put you in remote places, but sometimes the first miles can be busy, especially during peak summer months. Trail runners can be quiet and quickly sneak up on people. Let other trail users know when you're approaching well before overtaking them. A simple, "Hi, coming up on your left," is an easy way to give a heads-up. Allow plenty of space, and slow down as necessary. Also pay attention for animals, other runners, and on some trails, bikes. Use extra caution passing mule trains. Slow down, don't run, move off the trail, and don't get between a pack animal and a drop-off. They are not used to the faster foot traffic and can spook.

No one has priority over other users on the trail. Let's all be nice.

WISDOM FROM THE WILDERNESS

Allan Pietrasanta

Allan Pietrasanta has been enjoying the delights of the Sierra Nevada for over 50 years during all four seasons of the sun. His hiking, skiing, running, climbing, and picnicking adventures have taken him all over the range. He is always looking forward to the next opportunity to get out and spend time above timberline.

Wilderness remains as wild as we leave it. Wilderness designation is the highest land use protection in the United States. Preservation of wilderness continues by simply leaving the land alone, safe from future development or significant impacts.

Running through this treasured terrain with as little impact as possible not only helps preserve wilderness character, but also provides an opportunity for a deeper experience in the mountains and within ourselves.

It happens every time I step onto a trail in the Sierra Nevada: I feel the beginning of yet another journey into a sacred place. The enchanted world of captivating meadows, spectacular peaks, and diverse flora and fauna unfolds as I head deeper into the high country where human presence is minimally marked by the trails and hardened campsites that allow us to travel easily in this wild and virtually unspoiled land.

In the expansive space of wilderness, self-reliance is key; an approach that allows us a truer connection to this unique landscape and its spiritual environmental harmony.

Wilderness asks little of us, and we can do the same by choosing to do things as simple as hopping from rock to rock when off-trail, lessening damage to fragile alpine plants.

Shut off and tune out your everyday digital existence. Instead, turn onto the delights of the Clark's Nutcracker's caw, the pika and marmot calls in the talus fields, the smell of Jeffrey and Whitebark Pine and the sounds of the wind through their branches. Take in the visual poetry of the delicate Elephant's Head flowers found in mountain meadows and seek the rare fragrance of the Polemonium on the high passes. As the sunlight and shadows dance and change throughout the day, let your mind wonder what beauty is just around the next crenelated ridge or hanging valley in this Range of Light.

Experiencing and appreciating the splendor of the Sierra Nevada are the first steps toward caring for and preserving it. Endeavor to set a good example for those who follow in your running steps. Let's all do our part to keep wilderness wild. Protect it, cherish it, and care for it.

USING THIS BOOK

TRAILS

The runs in this book follow a combination of designated hiking trails, unmaintained use-trails, and cross-country wayfinding. The difficulty, steepness, and exposure of these trails vary widely in runnability, surface, and quality. The trails can be any combination of smooth, dusty, sandy, rocky, snowy, etc. Routes are marked with signposts or cairns, or sometimes not at all.

Note: Run every route in this book and your feet will touch less than two miles of asphalt.

Here's what you'll run on:

DIRT ROADS

While the majority of miles in this book follow singletrack, every now and again you'll run on a wider gravel or rocky surface, OHV road (off-highway vehicle), doubletrack, or dirt-bike trail.

USE TRAIL

Not an official trail, but people use it. These can be faint or indistinct, created by wear or tire marks. Use trails also change and move based on conditions and usage trends.

CROSS COUNTRY

Not on an established trail, or even a use trail. Sometimes the routes in this book go cross-country to connect official trails. Cross-country running takes some attention for navigation and route finding. The GPX tracks are key for direction, but off-trail route finding still requires experience and some savvy to safely navigate backcountry passes and peaks. If you are not experienced off trail, consider putting in the time on easier runs to hone your Sierra skills.

DG

Decomposed Granite. This is just what it sounds like, granite that's broken down. Somewhere between gravel and sand, DG is part of what makes running Sierra trails so good. But DG can roll like ball-bearings over hard or wet surfaces, and it's one reason you might consider that pair of gaiters.

SCREE

Scree is an intermediate-sized rock surface, larger than pebbles and smaller than talus. It shifts and slides. Scree slopes can be tough work to go up, but *screeing*, or scree-skiing, may be the optimal mode down from many Sierra summits.

TALUS

Talus fields are made of bigger rocks and boulders, sometimes stable but other times horrifyingly movable. To avoid terrible injury, every rock in a talus field should be considered loose until proven stable. Take talus seriously — and if it's new to you, keep in mind that it gets easier the more you do it.

SCRAMBLE

Scrambling is what you do when your hands are employed to help out your feet. It often comes near summits and might include exposure (fall consequences). Some of the runs include Class 2 and 3 scrambles.

US Grading System
  Class 1: Normal walking or hiking.
  Class 2: More difficult hiking that sometimes requires using your hands.
  Class 3: Sustained use of hands, often with serious exposure.
  Class 4: Difficult scrambling where a fall could be fatal. Ropes often used.
  Class 5: Technical rock climbing where even most experts use a rope.

CHOOSE YOUR ADVENTURE

We've rated the difficulty of each run on a scale of 1 to 5, from easier to harder. Difficulty takes into account distance, vertical gain, terrain, remoteness, exposure, and navigation. These ratings are subjective, represent opinions, and are relative to the other routes in this book only. It's just one way to help choose which run you're up for on any given day. For example, turn to page 223 if you want grueling vert, page 209 to get lost in the woods, or page 159 for a doubletrack that's made for conversation.

1. EASY

Shorter, less vertical gain, and tending to follow well-defined paths, these runs don't go off into the big mountains. There can still be some route finding and following of faint use-trails. Access tends to be easier and you won't spend all day out. The level of challenge can vary in this category from a flat 3-mile loop along the Bishop Canal to a steeper climb of Tungsten Peak. These low-commitment runs are good training repeaters, active rest days, bad-weather backups, or bonus shakeouts while you're in the area for one of the bigger routes.

2. MODERATE

These are a bit longer, with a bit more vertical gain, and on singletrack or mountain trails with smoother footing. Usually straightforward to navigate, often on forest or desert trails over lower passes and lower-angled climbs. These runs give you a taste of what's required to undertake the more challenging and committed routes. Mount Starr and Summit Lake, for example, are great tests before moving on to harder runs.

3. HARD

These runs usually have sections of smooth running, but are also going to have some technical footing. With a significant amount of vertical (sometimes 4000+ feet), they'll often add the challenge of altitude and potential exposure. Route examples: Boundary Peak and Mount Langley.

4. VERY HARD

These trails are getting rougher. They may require more navigation plus experience moving on talus and scree. Sections may be exposed with light scrambling. These runs generally have big elevation gain and head into remote areas. Route examples: Cloudripper and Mount Tyndall.

5. NAILS

Running these trails requires high fitness, technical skill, backcountry navigation, and commitment. The trail is more technical and exposed, might cross steep talus or scree, and may require scrambling. These runs are long, have big elevation gain, and may take you to wilder, remote areas without an easy way to bail. Sudden change in the weather can make the route difficult or dangerous. Good judgment and alpine experience necessary. Route examples: Rae Lakes and Lamarck to Piute Pass.

FAST PACKING

For some runners, these distances and elevation gains may be too much for a single day. For others, too short. Modifying the route or schedule creates an opportunity for a fast-packing trip. The difference between fast-packing and backpacking comes down to comfort. Fast-packing emphasizes long days of moving with minimal overnight gear, little comfort, and less room for error. Backpacking might include abundant comfort and lugging the weight that goes along with it.

RUNNING MODE

Many runs in this book follow smooth, flowing trails weaving through forests. Others climb steeply up exposed slopes, traverse talus, and plummet down scree. Some wander cross-country to connect peaks or passes. Often our favorite runs combine as many modes as possible. We've characterized five types of trail mode:

CRUISER

Non-technical running on a smooth-ish trail surface, ideally with gentle curves. You can shift into auto pilot, focus on form, stride out, enjoy the view, pretty much not pay attention too much to what's underfoot.

STEEP

Anything with a slope greater than mule-grade is where "steep" begins. Hiking these sections can be more energy efficient than running. Steep is relative.

TECHNICAL

Requires attentive footwork, focus, and sometimes your hands so you don't crash to the ground. Scree and talus or just gnarly, rooted, abundantly rocky trails are considered technical.

ADVENTURE

Most likely off-trail in the backcountry, where the miles are slow and the terrain serves up challenges in the form of talus, route finding, and maybe some scrambling.

EXPOSED

This means that the consequences of a fall are likely to be severe. Move deliberately and don't go up anything you wouldn't be comfortable coming back down.

ROUTE

This is pretty self explanatory, but each type of route has its own benefits. There's a suggested direction to run loops and lollipops based on the footing or terrain being better suited for uphill or downhill running, and sometimes the quality of the views. The direction you choose to do these runs can make a huge difference in the amount of running you do.

LOOP

Loops are perfect. Same start and finish, but every step in between is new.

LOLLIPOP

Like a loop, but with the added benefit of seeing part of the route from both directions. There's minimal repetition, but a sense of comfort in the familiarity, especially at the end of a long day out.

OUT-AND-BACK

You know exactly what to expect on the back. This can be a relief. Or a curse.

POINT-TO-POINT

Point-to-point runs can feel the most like a journey ... but then again, you need to plan a way to get back to point A from point B.

BEYOND THE BOOK

FIXES AND UPDATES

It's hard to believe we'd make a mistake, but if you find something in this book that needs updating, please help out future editions. Let us know at info@wolverinepublishing.com

WANT EVEN MORE?

To stay current on route changes and explore even more trails, visit the online resource: sierratrailruns.com

PREPARATION FOR SIERRA MOUNTAIN RUNNING

Scott Johnston

Scott Johnston is one of the founders and head coach at Uphill Athlete, the foremost training and education resource for mountain sport athletes. Along with Steve House, Scott co-wrote two of the most important books for mountain sport athletes; *Training for the New Alpinism: A Manual for the Climber as Athlete* and *Training for the Uphill Athlete*, along with Kilian Jornet.

To be the most ready you can be for your mountain running goals you need a plan. That plan needs to address the various and unique demands involved in this type of activity. Here's a look at Sierra specific demands and suggested training tools that we at Uphill Athlete have found to be especially helpful.

1. Many of the popular Sierra runs are going to involve days of 6 or more hours of constant movement.
Solution: Improving your endurance will help keep you moving for those long days with less fatigue.

2. The rough terrain, poor footing, and great elevation change will require more fatigue-resistant legs than it will speed.
Solution: Improving running-specific strength in the legs and hips will help protect you from injury and will build fatigue resistance for days with lots of vertical gain and loss.

3. You won't be running while traversing scree slopes or boulder hopping in talus fields. But, being able to move comfortably through this challenging terrain can keep you safe and cut precious hours off your day.

Solution: Develop better agility and balance so you can move comfortably over rough terrain when the footing is far from ideal.

IMPROVING ENDURANCE

These suggestions are just the tip. An excellent source for a deep dive into this subject can be found at UphillAthlete.com or in the book, Training for the Uphill Athlete.

Your muscles have two primary ways of producing the energy to propel you on the trail. One is the aerobic metabolic pathway which is a complex set of chemical reactions that break down both fat and carbohydrates in the presence of oxygen (aerobically). The other is known as the anaerobic or glycolytic metabolic pathway (anaerobic because it does not involve oxygen and glycolytic because it can only break down carbohydrates). Because of several factors explained in the sources mentioned above, the more of the energy you need that can be produced using the aerobic pathway the better your endurance will be.

- The aerobic pathway can meet the energy demands of low to moderate intensity work.
- The anaerobic pathway is best utilized to meet the energy demands of high intensity work.

The aerobic pathway is easily trained and is one of humans' most adaptable systems. That's because humans evolved as hunter-gatherers who needed to be able to keep moving at relatively slow paces for hours on end and be able to go days without a meal. Proper training will increase the capacity of the aerobic pathway's ability to produce that vital propulsive force at a faster rate.

Similarly there are training methods to improve the anaerobic capacity.

The problem is that training to improve the capacity of either of the systems necessarily reduces the capacity of the other system. So, you are left with a choice to make. Focus on building aerobic capacity or anaerobic capacity. Knowing that the aerobic pathway is best suited to producing energy for low to moderate intensity exercise and the activity you are training for involves hour upon hour of relatively slow running or fast hiking should help make your choice much easier.

This does not mean that training of the anaerobic system plays no part in improving endurance. It just means that it plays a minor role. A very minor role in fact. A well con-structed training plan that targets improv-ing your ability to handle big days means anaerobic pathway training will make up no more than 5% of your overall training time.

How do you know which of these paths is the dominant energy producer? There are a number of ways, but one very simple way is to check to see if you can speak in complete sentences. If you find yourself short of breath and able to get out few words at a time, you are training too hard to optimize the development of aerobic capacity.

The aerobic system responds best to a high volume of low to moderate intensity work. This is a case where more is better. It is why the most successful marathon runners run 100 miles or more per week.

Keep in mind that a significant portion of your Sierra mountain "run" may in fact be done walking. Long, steep climbs will necessitate even the strongest runner shift to walking. The altitude, which we'll address later, may force you to walk more than you are used to if you live and train at lower elevations. You should include walking in your training program. Walking and running have a lot in common, but being good at one does not mean you are good at the other. If you don't want to have to dawdle along at 30 minutes per mile when you are forced to walk, you need to work on developing the technique of walking fast. This should be practiced during some of your longer runs in training.

If you are living in a "terrain challenged" area you will want to search out some options for your run/hikes. These might take some effort to suss out but will pay off. Stair machines are incredibly effective at improving your ability to hike steeply uphill. Incline trainers (most treadmills go to only 15% grade) that can go to 20-30% grade are also very useful. Other reasonable substitutes for mountainous terrain are stadium stairs and fire stairs in tall buildings. Stairs are better than the machine methods mentioned above because you can go back down the stairs. There is a very specific and useful type of strength gained by descending stairs. As a last resort one can step up onto and down from a box or bench.

IMPROVING FATIGUE RESISTANCE AND DURABILITY

While the aerobic capacity provides the base of support for long days and shortens recovery time between big efforts, your legs will take a beating. There are some good strategies to help this muscular beat down.

Long duration running even at low intensity results in a special kind of fatigue that will leave your legs feeling heavy and dead. Some of that fatigue will be reduced by consuming calories during the run. But, the real killer is fatigue of the central nervous system (CNS). The CNS is responsible for the millions of electrical signals being sent to all your muscles. The millions of repetitions of the same movement patterns achieved during a multi-hour run reduces the effectiveness of those same nerve impulses. The muscles fire less strongly, with less efficiency, and in a less coordinated way. If you have ever run for several hours you have no doubt experienced this phenomenon. CNS fatigue has been shown in studies to be the most significant form of fatigue experienced by ultra runners. Unfortunately, it won't be helped much by consuming more calories during your run.

Most people will tell you that to build this kind of fatigue resistance can only be done by accumulating a high volume of running/hiking miles on steep mountainous terrain. This makes intuitive sense and is true. If you train in a very specific manner that models the demands of the activity you are training for, you will improve fatigue resistance and durability. But, there are a couple of problems with this:

- First, many people who aspire to do mountain runs are in fact "terrain challenged." Living a long way from mountains precludes regular training like this. While occasionally getting on mountain trails is better than nothing it won't bring you the level of fatigue resistance you need.
- Second, this high volume of mountain running carries with it a significant global fatigue load (due to the energy requirements) and increases your risk of injury. Even if you have the energy and are injury proof, the time required to accumulate a big volume of mountain running in training is a luxury most of us don't have.

We've got another way that we have found to be as effective as the above method but without the downsides of time and global fatigue. That is using a method called Muscular Endurance (ME) training. ME training focuses on the main locomotive muscles and taxes them almost to the point of exhaustion using a series of special exercises. We have written in copious detail about this training method that we have used with tremendous success from rank beginner mountain runners to some of the best in the business. I encourage you to read either the chapter on Muscular Endurance in *Training For the Uphill Athlete,* or the article *At Home Muscular Endurance Workout with Progression* on UphillAthlete.com, which includes instructions and details of the workout moving from challenging to very hard over the course of many weeks.

Don't be surprised if these ME workouts leave you quite stiff and sore for a couple of days. If you are new to this style of training, dial back the intensity for the first two to three workouts until you get the hang of it. You can also start with a reduced number of sets for each exercise.

This is a very potent form of training. But, like anything that packs a big punch, it needs to be handled with care.

IMPROVING AGILITY & BALANCE

This is another area where having access to similar challenges as you will encounter on your Sierra run will be a big help. If you run mostly on paved surfaces or smooth trails you may be developing great fitness, but will not be developing an element of training that allows you to move at a better speed and more economically (using less energy) across very rough ground. Some of the trails you'll run in the Sierra will be covered with scree (golf-ball- to grapefruit-sized rock). Other areas may actually have no trail and you will need to hop from boulder to boulder for progress. The consequences of having poor agility in these situations may be much worse than just having to slow down. A twisted ankle from a misstep in scree or a miscalculated hop in a boulder field could lead to a nasty gouge or even a broken leg.

We've developed an eight-week (you will progress at your own speed) agility, strength and mobility program for mountain athletes. The video-based Mountain Fit At-Home Strength Program on UphillAthlete.com is guided by an excellent instructor. The program progresses through four levels from fairly easy to quite challenging. It focuses on core strength, single leg stability, and balance which are paramount to developing agility.

Some alternatives to this program are to set up a small obstacle course that includes small round boulders you can hop on and off of. You can use a picnic bench to jump onto and down from. Run in a dry river bed covered with small stones. As you can see this is going to require some ingenuity on your part. Use an interval training protocol for this type of training where you go pretty hard across your challenge for 2-3 minutes and then rest for the same time. Repeat this five to six times in a workout. This could be incorporated into your regular trail runs one or two times per week.

Besides these three main areas of focus, adjusting to altitude is also a key component to having a good run in the Sierra.

ALTITUDE

Altitude plays a big role in these Sierra runs. Most of these runs take place between 10,500 feet and 14,000 feet above sea level. If you do not have a way to pre-acclimate to these elevations, be prepared to suffer and be significantly slower than normal. The most common comment from athletes when arriving at higher altitudes is that they feel like they have lost their fitness. While you might wonder if you did something wrong with your training that has left you feeling like you have one lung, it is much more likely that a sudden drop in performance when you go to higher elevations is simply a lack of acclimatization.

If you live at low elevations, acclimatization is probably going to be the biggest challenge you face when you arrive. It takes many weeks for the body to fully acclimate to these elevations. The first thing you will notice is an elevated heart rate both at rest and when exercising. The second annoying thing you'll notice is poor sleep quality. In a few days you will begin to feel a little bit better as some of the body's systems adapt faster than others. But, you'll still notice a significant drop in performance that might necessitate walking more on the trails. After about two weeks up at altitude you'll probably see a very noticeable performance gain over your first days' nadir. Full acclimatization happens after you've been up there for a couple of months.

This does not mean you can't do these high runs. Just don't expect to be as speedy as you are at home. You'll need to be more patient.

Maximizing both performance and experience in the Sierra requires some preparation. Actively including the appropriate training is going to make for an overall better run.

BETWEEN THE PINES

MOUNT LANGLEY

MOUNT LANGLEY

BETWEEN THE PINES: LONE PINE

DISTANCE:

22-mile lollipop, clockwise

GAIN:
4840 feet

DIFFICULTY:
●●●○○

HIGH POINT: 14,032 ft Mount Langley
LOW POINT: 10,060 ft Cottonwood Lakes Trailhead

PROFILE:

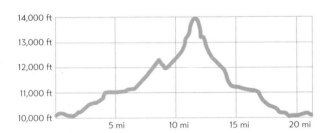

OBJECTIVE: Peak
RUNNING: 75%
MODE: Cruiser, Technical
SEASON: June–October
PERMIT: No

ACCESS: Cottonwood Lakes Trailhead
36°27'11.3"N 118°10'11.5"W
Pit toilet, campground

APPROACH: From Highway 395 in Lone Pine, turn west onto Whitney Portal Road. After 3 miles, turn south onto Horseshoe Meadows Road and switchback up for 20 miles before a right turn toward the Cottonwood Lakes Trailhead parking.

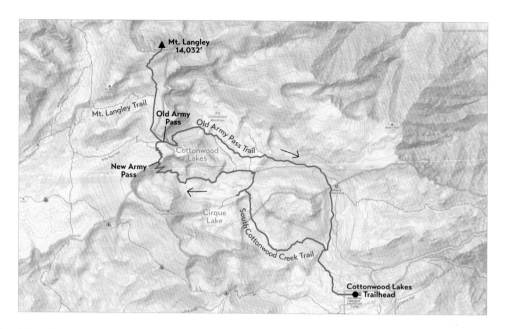

THE ROUTE

Mount Langley is California's southernmost 14er. It might also be the friendliest for runners. The trail starts high and wanders, on what you can barely consider uphill, through forest and meadows, before a steeper ramp to the summit. What it lacks in vertical gain it more than makes up for in mile after mile of smooth running.

- Starting out on the Cottonwood Lakes Trail, you might notice that running a 14er seems surprisingly easy. That's because, as you might also notice, the trail is angling gently downhill. Tuck away that observation until 20 miles later, when you're making the slightly uphill finish on tired legs. Don't settle too much into the flow before finding the unmarked left turnoff a little over 1 mile in, just past the south fork of Cottonwood Creek. After that you can switch into low-angle running mode along easy forest miles that connect to New Army Pass Trail.

- Another 3 miles lead beside the south sides of Cottonwood Lakes (#1 and #2), Long Lake, and High Lake before gaining the long switchbacks to New Army Pass. Head up and over the pass, and after a short descent, briefly cut cross-country to meet the Old Army Pass Trail and begin the 2-mile out-and-

back to the summit along the south slope of Mount Langley. The way up is marked by impossible-to-miss cairns. Before the top, the gently angled DG trail gets you breathing harder. It's slow going up, but it'll be soft and speedy back down.

- Wow. That's a view. After hunkering down in the mountain-top wind, start that super downhill back to the junction at Old Army Pass.

- Rolling over Old Army Pass, follow the traverse and steep but short switchbacks down to Cottonwood Lake #4 and angle between Cottonwood Lakes #4 and #5.

- From there, toward #3. The long run out stays on Cottonwood Lakes Trail, passing through pretty meadows and golden-barked foxtail pines into lodgepole forest.

The Draw So much low-angle running, and tagging a 14er with one of the most dramatic views of the Whitney Group.

Don't Miss The very first turn off the main trail. A little over 1 mile in, just past the south fork of Cottonwood Creek you need to find the unmarked trail that winds through the forest and connects to New Army Trail further along.

Something Extra Five miles in, the trail comes to a T. The route goes right onto the Cirque Lake Trail, but if you make a left you'll find a beautiful little lake with a view out to Langley.

Old vs New Old Army Pass is the normal route up. It's slightly shorter, which also makes it more traveled. The advantage of taking New Army for the ascent is that it's lower angle and the runnable miles pass quickly.

This peak is not Mount Whitney In 1871, Clarence King and Paul Pinson thought they made the first ascent of Mount Whitney, a belief they held for two full years before it was corrected. Really, they were on top of Langley where they had found a cairn with an arrow.

Pining The sculpted trees around the meadows are Foxtail Pines. This rare tree with dark purple cones is found only at high elevations in California.

In View The Whitney Group, Mount Williamson, Great Western Divide.

TRAIL BETA

- Snow and ice can linger on Old Army Pass. New Army Pass (south facing) makes Langley accessible when the more direct line, Old Army Pass (northeast facing), is snowy or icy. While we prefer a clockwise loop in dry conditions, consider running counterclockwise early in the season to go uphill through lingering snow and ice on the steeper Old Army trails.

- Because Mount Langley is so far south, in low snow years it's often possible to do this run earlier or later in the season.

- Loop it without the final out-and-back to the summit for an excellent altitude training that's all a runnable grade.

- **GEAR:** Gaiters.

ALABAMA HILLS

ALABAMA HILLS

BETWEEN THE PINES: LONE PINE

DISTANCE:

6-mile loop, counterclockwise

GAIN:
950 feet

DIFFICULTY:
●○○○○

HIGH POINT: 4848 ft
LOW POINT: 4478 ft

PROFILE:

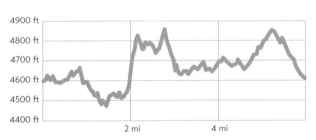

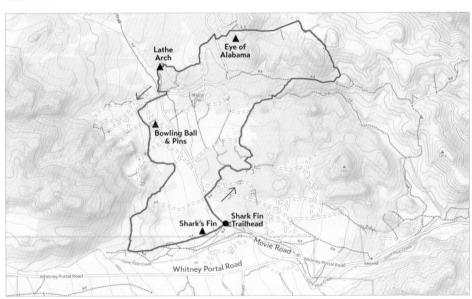

OBJECTIVE: Running
RUNNING: 100%
MODE: Cruiser
SEASON: Year round
PERMIT: No

ACCESS: Shark Fin Trailhead
36°35′56.0″N
118°07′04.9″W
Various port-a pots
around the Alabama Hills

APPROACH: From 395 in
Lone Pine, head west on
Whitney Portal Road.
Turn right onto Movie
Road. Parking is a half
mile down on the left.

THE ROUTE

Welcome to the Alabama Hills Highlight Tour. Starting out on Movie Road, the route follows a mix of dirt roads and the rolling Alabama Hills and Arch Loop Trails. This area has been the set for lots of Hollywood films. It's full of curious boulders, and you'll pass between such famous formations as Eye of Alabama, Lathe Arch, Bowling Ball and Pins, and Shark's Fin. While winding through the rocks close up, you'll have even bigger views rising to the Sierra giants above.

TRAIL BETA

Top off this short run with a full breakfast plus a piece of pie at the Alabama Hills Cafe & Bakery.

MOUNT WHITNEY / TUMANGUYA

MOUNT WHITNEY / TUMANGUYA

BETWEEN THE PINES: LONE PINE

DISTANCE:

21-mile out-and-back

↑ GAIN:
↓ 6650 feet

DIFFICULTY:
●●●○○

HIGH POINT: 14,505 ft Mount Whitney
LOW POINT: 8360 ft Whitney Portal

PROFILE:

OBJECTIVE: Peak
RUNNING: 75%
MODE: Cruiser, Technical
SEASON: Off-peak permit season
PERMIT: Yes. Permit necessary to enter the Whitney Zone.

ACCESS: Whitney Portal Trailhead
   36°35'12.7"N 118°14'24.5"W
   Toilets, camping, food

APPROACH: From 395 in Lone Pine, head west on Whitney
   Portal Road. Wind to the end of the road and park at the
   Whitney Portal Trailhead.

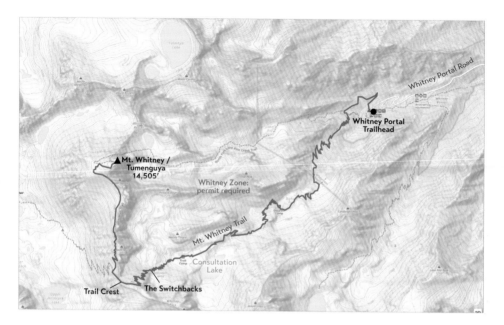

THE ROUTE

You can't run any higher than here in the Lower 48. That's big bragging rights for what's really a pretty straightforward, well-worn, and mule-graded endeavor. The trail itself is smooth and runnable — if you can pull it off in the off-season and avoid the mess of permits and people.

- From the Upper Trailhead, switchbacks through the forest gain elevation quickly. The first 3 miles are smooth and soft, a perfect running trail leading to the signposted Whitney Zone. From there, it's necessary to have a permit to continue.

- Just after Trail Camp, you hit the infamous switchbacks. The trail is steeper, and that's right, makes more than a few quick switchbacks to gain the Trail Crest. The switchbacks can hold snow and ice late into the season.

- You'll follow along the west side of the line of peaks you've aimed at until now. Mount Muir, Aiguille Junior, Aiguille du Paquoir, Third Needle, and Keeler Needle are all just off your right side. All the Aiguilles might make you think you're in the French Alps ... but then the trail wouldn't be mule grade; you'd be going straight up.

- The final steps to the summit aren't steep or exposed, but may pass a little slower thanks to the lack of O2. Welcome to the summit of Mount Whitney. At the top, you get to look down on all the summits you still have to do.

- As a reminder, you're only halfway there. Save time to make your way back down and savor some of the best running trails in the Sierra. And remember those first miles up? They're the perfect finish.

The Draw Highest Point in the Lower 48. And also, surprisingly flowy trails for running.

Don't Miss No doubt you'll be hungry after this one. Head straight down into Lone Pine and scan the street corners: taco-truck tacos at the end of this big day are the best tacos ever.

Whitney Portal Store Famous for their enormous pancakes and I-made-it-to-the-summit-of-Mount-Whitney celebratory burgers. Breakfast and dinner if you can squeeze the run in between opening hours. Or stay an extra day for the much-needed refuel.

Fisherman's Peak The mountain was almost called "Fisherman's Peak," since its "first ascent" (first known ascent by Europeans) was by a group of fishermen in 1873. The USGS had given the mountain its current name in 1864, for Californian geologist Josiah Whitney, and stuck with it.

Tumanguya Before all that, the Nuumu (Paiute) and Newe (Shoshone) named this mountain Tumanguya, meaning "very old man."

In View Everything lower.

TRAIL BETA

- To go during quota season, May 1 to November 1, you need a permit earned through the lottery, which opens in February. Using a lottery system months in advance to get a permit for a day run is pretty annoying.

- For a better experience, go in the off-season. From November to April, the hoops are easier to jump through, and you can get a permit on shorter notice. You just might get the summit and the whole trail up to it all to yourself. The downside, of course, is off-season trail conditions. Figure out the snowpack and know what you are capable of.

- Be sure you're carrying sufficient water before heading for the switchbacks. There's a lot of elevation before the chance to refill on the way back down.

- **GEAR:** Pack your microspikes if you're uncertain about snow and ice on the switchbacks. And a headlamp, just in case.

MOUNT TYNDALL

MOUNT TYNDALL

BETWEEN THE PINES: INDEPENDENCE

DISTANCE:

24.5-mile out-and-back

GAIN:
9170 feet

DIFFICULTY:
●●●●●

HIGH POINT: 14,025 ft Mount Tyndall
LOW POINT: 6300 ft Shepherd Pass Trailhead

PROFILE:

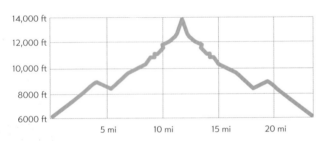

OBJECTIVE: Peak
RUNNING: 65%
MODE: Cruiser, Steep, Technical, Adventure, Exposed
SEASON: June–October
PERMIT: No

ACCESS: Shepherd Pass Trailhead
    36°43'38.5"N 118°16'43.0"W
    No facilities

APPROACH: From Highway 395 in Independence, turn west
    onto Market Street (Onion Valley Road). After 4 miles,
    turn south onto Foothill Road. Continue past the Pack
    Trailhead and turn right onto a rough dirt road, following
    signs to Shepherd Pass Trailhead.

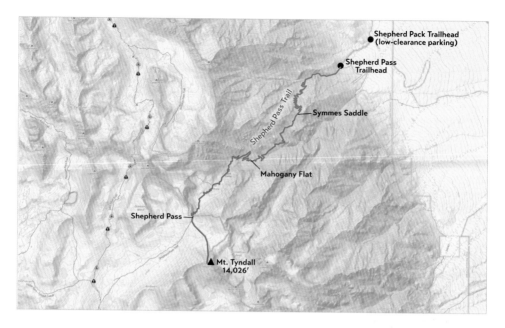

Shepherd Pack Trailhead
(low-clearance parking)

Shepherd Pass
Trailhead

Shepherd Pass Trail

Symmes Saddle

Mahogany Flat

Shepherd Pass

▲ Mt. Tyndall
14,026'

THE ROUTE

Any hiker will bemoan the drudgery of Shepherd Pass, but for a runner, this might just be the greatest singletrack in the entire Sierra. Besides miles of marvelous DG, this run tags another California 14er and gains loads of vert. That's right, you're in for the Mount Tyndall marathon.

- With no easy warm-up, this run starts gaining from the get-go. The Shepherd Pass Trail makes a couple dozen switchbacks on the way to Symmes Saddle where it pops out of the forest.

- After a short traverse from the saddle, you'll suddenly find yourself running downhill for much longer than feels acceptable. Fun for now, but you know this will need to be reversed on the way out, with 20 miles and well over 8000 feet in the legs. Tuck that away for now and focus on climbing to Mahogany Flat through a pretty pine zone. Soft, low-angled DG gives way to steeper trail just before arriving at Shepherd Pass.

- From Shepherd Pass, you finally get your first look at the tilted Mount Tyndall and your way up it. Angle around the west side of the lake toward the imposing rubble ramp, aiming for the defined rib on its north flank.

- From here it's short, steep, and slow with no clearly discernible route. Navigate up boulders and slabs to the ridge, then boulder-hop to the summit. Be sure not to go up anything you won't be comfortable coming back down.

- Off the summit, across the plateau, and back to Shepherd Pass. From the pass all the way back down is possibly the very best trail running in all of the Sierra. Soft, fast DG for a long, long way is only briefly disrupted by the morning's fun downhill, a discouraging bit of up. Thanks to the creamy curves and even trail, the final miles count down quicker than you'd expect on scrambled legs.

Mount Tyndall itself is one giant slab. Bring your sticky-rubber running shoes and monster calves.

The Draw It's a big day, combining quality running on a well-worn trail into the backcountry with an easy mountaineering scramble to the peak.

Don't Miss The true summit. Following the north rib, you'll frequently think you are almost there, only to see more mountain looming above. Once you reach the short ridge traverse, two false summits jab you with minor disappointment, even though you have only a few more minutes to go.

Tyndall Turnaround Skip the peak bagging and turn back at Shepherd Pass. It's a great run itself without the slow scramble up to the summit.

Close to Second Mount Williamson (14,379 feet), California's second-highest peak, stands beside Mount Tyndall, offering another even longer and higher option from Shepherd Pass.

In View Mount Williamson, Mount Whitney, Kaweah Peaks.

TRAIL BETA

- In a low-clearance vehicle you might consider parking at the Shepherd Pack Trail and join the Shepherd Pass Trail, adding an extra 1.5-mile jog on each end of the route.

- Carefully pick through the sometimes loose boulders on the north rib for the short but tedious up and down Tyndall, using extra caution to protect anyone below from falling rocks. Class 3 scrambling.

- The northwest ridge is an easier but much longer way up Tyndall. It's the obvious ridge seen from Shepherd Pass if the steep north rib isn't your thing. Class 2.

- The final steep steps to Shepherd Pass, as well as the north rib, can hold snow and ice. You're headed high, so be prepared.

- **GEAR:** Poles, gaiters, headlamp.

Kim Strom making her way down to Shepherd Pass after descending Mt. Tyndall.

MOUNT GOULD

MOUNT GOULD FROM KEARSARGE PASS

DISTANCE:

12-mile out-and-back

GAIN:
4050 feet

DIFFICULTY:

●●○○○

HIGH POINT: 13,012 ft Mount Gould
LOW POINT: 9200 ft Kearsarge Pass Trailhead

PROFILE:

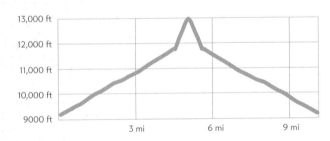

OBJECTIVE: Peak
RUNNING: 75%
MODE: Cruiser, Technical
SEASON: May–November
PERMIT: No

ACCESS: Kearsarge Pass Trailhead
    36°46'21.8"N 118°20'25.1"W
    Pit toilet

APPROACH: Along Highway 395 in Independence, turn west
    onto Market Street, which becomes Onion Valley Road.
    Parking is about 15 miles uphill from Independence at the
    end of Onion Valley Road.

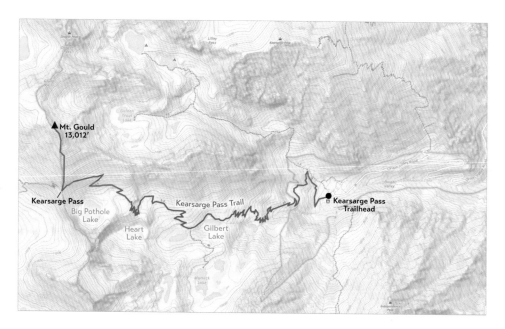

THE ROUTE

This is the ideal intro to Sierra out-and-back peak running. Unlike a lot of Eastside runs, this one's got a shot of instant gratification. It starts off high, is quick to the pass on a gently angled trail, and topped off with an easy scramble to the blocky summit of Mount Gould. Reverse your out with a fast and flowing back.

- From the Kearsarge Pass Trailhead, you've got good running and great views from the get-go. Following the low-angle, wide-sweeping switchbacks, you'll find this either the perfect trail to tune up your uphill ... or annoyingly just low-angle enough that you can't quite justify dropping into power-hike mode.

- At 2 miles in it might seem too early to take a break, but there are some tempting flat rocks above Gilbert Lake where you might stop for a quick refuel — or remember these for the way out.

- The switchbacks are a bit steeper above Heart Lake, but then lessen to a false flat above treeline all the way up to Kearsarge Pass (11,709 feet). From the pass, you are looking down to the Kearsarge Basin, toward the passage of the Pacific Crest and John Muir trails, and westward to the wild views of the Sierra Nevada backcountry. Mount Gould is directly north along the Sierra Crest, the unmarked seam of the John Muir Wilderness and Kings Canyon National Park.

- The way up to Mount Gould is worn in enough to be mostly obvious, and leads to a final bouldery scramble to the summit. Class 2 with an awesome view.

- Rewind to the pass and be prepared to break new speed barriers on the smooth, low-angle descent back to the trailhead. Maybe hit up those flat rocks by Gilbert Lake for a final break before you get all the way down.

The Draw For trail runners, Kearsarge is the easiest pass over the Sierra Crest. Much of the climb is runnable without destroying the legs and lungs, leaving plenty in the tank for the fun scramble up Mount Gould.

Don't Miss Big Pothole Lake. This appropriately named lake dips deep below its University Peak backdrop, and stays iced over late into the summer.

Something Extra If you want more — a lot more — try the Rae Lakes Run over three passes: Baxter, Glen, and Kearsarge (see page 76).

Local Lore The shortest way across the Sierra Nevada, road to road, is from Road's End in Kings Canyon to Onion Valley over Kearsarge Pass. At only 21 miles, following Bubb's Creek Trail, you might just run this from eastside to westside, or westside to eastside, in less time than it takes to drive the 350 miles between the trailheads.

Thru (Hitch) Hikers At the trailhead, don't be surprised if there's a line of smelly, shaggy, skinny thru hikers seeking a ride down to Independence for a resupply.

In View University Peak, Kearsarge Pinnacles, Mount Bago, Rae Lakes.

TRAIL BETA

- Because the trail gets south-facing sun it can be a hot one, but that also extends its runnability into the shoulder seasons — typically May to November. Just be sure Onion Valley Road is open.

- Use those shoulder seasons. Kearsarge Pass Trail can be crowded in mid summer, so go before or after the pack animals, mosquitos, and the majority of trail trompers. You'll also beat the summer heat.

- GEAR: Gloves and a wind shirt. It's always fricking cold above the pass.

Climbing the south ridge of Mount Gould, with Big Pothole Lake and University Peak behind.

RAE LAKES

RAE LAKES

BETWEEN THE PINES: INDEPENDENCE

DISTANCE:

26-mile point-to-point

↑ GAIN:
9340 feet

↓ DESCENT:
6700 feet

DIFFICULTY:
●●●●●

HIGH POINT: **12,300 ft Baxter Pass**

LOW POINT: **6000 ft Baxter Pass Trailhead**

PROFILE:

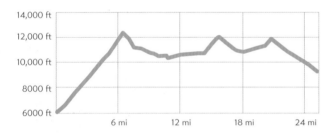

OBJECTIVE: Three Passes: Baxter, Glen, Kearsarge
RUNNING: 50%
MODE: Cruiser, Technical, Adventure
SEASON: June–October
PERMIT: No. But if you do it in 2 days, a permit is required for overnight.

ACCESS: Baxter Pass Trailhead 36°50'41.5"N 118°17'51.5"W
No facilities

APPROACH: Two miles north of Independence, turn west off Highway 395 onto Fish Hatchery Road. Take the right fork onto North Oak Creek Road and 5 miles to the trailhead at the end of the road.

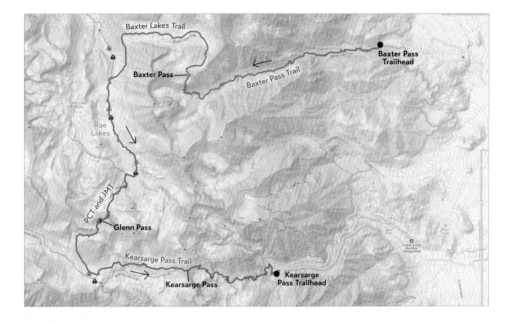

THE ROUTE

Maybe the longest 26 miles in the whole Sierra, this is one for the very fit, or for the moderately fit with plenty of time. When we finally reached the finish, we were sure we'd done double the stats. This run takes in three passes, including the grueling Baxter Pass, but it also allows you to run a spectacular section of the JMT/PCT through the Rae Lakes Basin and finish with the fast and flowing descent of Kearsarge Pass to Onion Valley.

- Twenty-six miles of adventure suffering begin with the climb over Baxter Pass, a relentless, 6000-foot grind in about 7 miles. The Baxter Pass Trail is unmaintained and requires a bit of bushwhacking. In less than 3 miles you'll cross the creek from the south to the north bank, just before the downed trees seem impassable. The way is faint, but if you're not on some faint trail you're off route.

- Back, back, and still further back into the canyon — it's about 6 miles of looking at the same, unchanging view. Finally you'll turn from that straight line and up steeper switchbacks on the loose scree to Baxter Pass.

- The beige and gray south side of the pass rolls over to rusty red, black, and gold stripes — a sudden inferno. But the run down from Baxter Pass to Baxter Lake is about as good as a steep descent can be. Then you're in for 4 miles of wayfinding. Patience and a sense of adventure is the best way through these miles. It's pretty slow wandering through the unmaintained, sparsely cairned connection from Baxter Lake to Dollar Lake, where you're not too unhappy about joining the highway of hikers on a shared section of the John Muir and Pacific Crest trails.

- From wild and desolate to the JMT/PCT parade, smooth miles and mindless navigation let you enjoy the gorgeous views in the Rae Lakes Basin. OK, it makes sense why so many people are on this trail. Lake after lake, open pine groves, pointed granite peaks — it's the essence of the Sierra.

- Glide along until you reach the imposing climb to Glen Pass, which turns out to be much shorter than it looks. Head up and over; Glen Pass is stellar on both sides.

- Cruising along, all gently downhill from Glen Pass, you'll leave the JMT/PCT at the junction before Bullfrog Lake for a last uphill to Kearsarge Pass. The final climb is gradual, leading into stretched-out hairpin switchbacks to the pass. Now it's all coasting, an easy-flowing descent to finish at Onion Valley.

The Draw Honestly, almost the whole first half of the trail is a grind, but sometimes, as runners, we like that. Two and a half of the three passes are incredible — OK, that ratio sounds better — and as a whole, the experience is unbelievably beautiful.

Don't miss An exit strategy. A) Park one car at the Kearsarge Pass Trailhead in Onion Valley before heading over to Baxter Pass Trailhead. B) Arrange a pickup for when you come out at Kearsarge. C) Hitch. Good luck!

Something Extra The Kearsarge Lakes are an inviting detour just briefly off route before the final pass.

Local Lore Rae Lakes is known as one of the most beautiful places in the Sierra. Doing this run in a single go is a quick way to get to some of the most loved views along the much longer PCT, JMT, and Rae Lakes Loop.

Why not reverse it? Sure, we thought about that. It seems logical to do less net gain, but the run down Kearsarge is such a satisfying finish that you've probably forgotten cursing your way up Baxter Pass. This direction, you move from scrappy to smooth — do you really want to end a long run by bushwacking your way down Bastard? You're welcome.

In View So many lakes. Mount Baxter, Diamond Peak, Mount Clarence King, Mount Cotter, Fin Dome, Painted Lady, Charlotte Dome, East Vidette, University Peak.

TRAIL BETA

- Make this route less about suffering and more about adventure.

- Get an early start. The way up to Baxter Pass can be hot.

- On the way up Baxter Pass, don't get suckered in by sucker trails.

- Avoid peak mosquito season and thunderstorms. Both can bite.

- Fastpack it. The extra gear slows things down a little, but you can spend a night near Rae Lakes. Bivy before the smooth running starts, and split this run into a 2-day fastpack adventure for more time to enjoy the views.

- GEAR: If overnighting, don't forget a permit, bear canister, and camp stuff.

CARDINAL MOUNTAIN

CARDINAL MOUNTAIN FROM TABOOSE PASS

BETWEEN THE PINES: BIG PINE

DISTANCE:

17-mile out-and-back

GAIN:
8130 feet

DIFFICULTY:

HIGH POINT: 13,396 ft Cardinal Mountain
LOW POINT: 5500 ft Taboose Pass Trailhead

PROFILE:

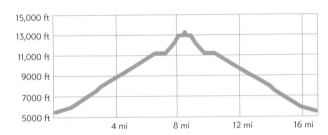

OBJECTIVE: Peak
RUNNING: 40%
MODE: Steep, Technical, Adventure, Exposed
SEASON: June–October
PERMIT: No

ACCESS: Taboose Pass Trailhead
   37°00'34.8"N 118°19'39.8"W
   No facilities

APPROACH: From Hwy 395, turn west on Aberdeen Station Road, which soon turns into Taboose Creek Road. With a few choices to make at the beginning, use your map to remain on the correct track. Follow this slow, jarring dirt road to its end at the trailhead (approximately 5.5 miles from the highway). High clearance is highly recommended.

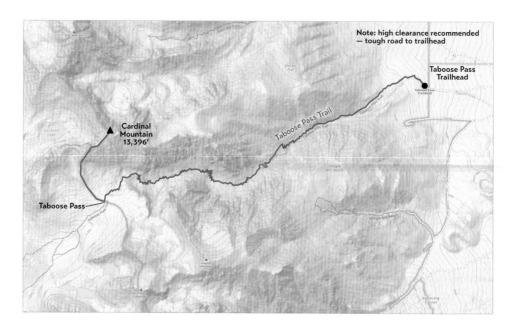

Note: high clearance recommended
— tough road to trailhead

Taboose Pass
Trailhead

Cardinal
Mountain
13,396'

Taboose Pass Trail

Taboose Pass

THE ROUTE

If you wake up feeling like a good hike, this is the run for you. From a fire-ravaged start through towering, golden-granite walls, and a steep talus climb to Cardinal Mountain, the Taboose Pass Trail gets more and more stunning as you gain elevation. If calling it a run is a bit of a stretch, we still felt like 40% running was enough to make the book. The place is just that good.

- The trail starts out gradually, winding through sage before entering Taboose Creek Canyon.

- After the first creek crossing, you're briefly in the forest. Under the triangular spire of Mount Goodale's north ridge, the creek spreads out between rocks, potentially the last reliable water source later in the season. Follow the trail over boulders and the open expanse to the top of the pass.

- From Taboose Pass, quit the trail and aim for the southwest ridge of Cardinal Mountain. Pick your way up steep talus and stacked rocks to a false summit. Sidle around the somewhat exposed southern slope to gain a saddle below the final 500 feet. Push through this last bit of talus for spectacular summit views over to Split Mountain's psychedelically striped south face, swirls of moraine straight down, and a rainbow of rock colors all around.

- When you've realized it's a long way down, return to the saddle where you have a choice to make: either play it safe and retrace your ascent route, or plunge straight down the steep and loose south chute on a conveyor belt of debris.

- Back at the pass, take a moment to empty your shoes and resume the trail. Then retrace the miles, watching the later light give new emphasis to spires and buttresses. Wrap up this long day with a soft and sandy descent aimed at the obvious red cinder cone. Finish with curves on the alluvial mile to the car.

The Draw Lots of vertical to a major pass and a mighty view from a less-frequented summit.

Don't Miss The red cinder cone in the valley below is part of the Aberdeen/Big Pine Volcanic Field, a zone of lava flows and cones from faults formed by the spreading of the Basin and Range Province.

Something Extra Baxter Honey, the sweet Owens Valley elixir, has been bottled here since 1875. The hives are clustered in the sage up and down the valley, with headquarters right by Tinemaha Creek. Pick up a jar of liquid gold Buckwheat or Wildflower honey at local bakeries and grocers.

Goliath As you stand on the summit of Cardinal Mountain, imagine following the ridgeline north for the next 8 days. Alone and unsupported. Connecting more than 60 peaks, with hairy exposure and more than 80,000 feet of climbing. In 2021, Vitaliy Musiyenko pulled off this gargantuan link-up of two sought-after alpine traverses, the Full Monty Palisade Traverse and the Full Evolution Crest Traverse, to create one Goliath Traverse.

Taboose Historically cultivated by the Nuumu (Paiute), the tuber of Tupusi (Taboose) grass provided a main crop and food source.

In View Split Mountain, Birch Mountain, Mount Tinemaha, Vennacher Needle, Mount Ruskin, Bench Lake, Arrow Peak.

TRAIL BETA

- With a low-elevation start and little shade, it pays to do this one early to beat the oppression of the sun.

- Consider full-length leg cover for the spiky plant-claws crowding the trail that are cumulative torture in shorts.

- Descending the unstable south gully is a quick line down, but unless you're confident in your steep-screeing skills, it's better to descend the way you came up.

- GEAR: Poles, gaiters, headlamp, and plenty of snacks for a long day.

Huffing and puffing to the summit of Cardinal Mountain in spring conditions.

MCMURRY MEADOWS

MCMURRY MEADOWS

BETWEEN THE PINES: BIG PINE

DISTANCE:

7-mile loop, counterclockwise

 GAIN:
1130 feet

DIFFICULTY:
●○○○○

HIGH POINT: 6070 ft

LOW POINT: 4960 ft Little Pine Creek

PROFILE:

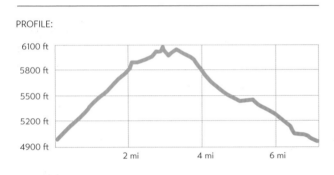

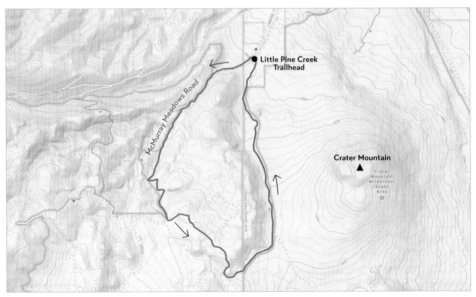

OBJECTIVE: Running
RUNNING: 100%
MODE: Cruiser
SEASON: Year round
PERMIT: No

ACCESS: McMurry Meadows Road
37°07'52.2"N 118°19'24.7"W
No facilities

APPROACH: From Highway 395 in Big Pine, turn west onto W Crocker Avenue, which becomes Glacier Lodge Road. After 2 miles, turn left onto McMurry Meadows Road. Park a mile further up the road at a righthand pullout.

THE ROUTE

Here's some easy running as long as it's not baking in the sun. It's all on gently rolling dirt roads, lined with flowering rabbitbrush. Not too long, and not much up, the loop explores the Big Pine volcanic field next to Crater Mountain. Besides the protruding red and black cinder cones, the views of Birch Mountain and Mount Tinemaha make a worthwhile stop to stretch your legs while you're making your way along the Eastside. Add an out-and-back up Crater Mountain if you don't mind interrupting the smooth running with some sharp volcanic rock and rattlesnakes underfoot.

TRAIL BETA

Finding the narrow crossing over Little Pine Creek to get started is the only navigational challenge of this loop, and even that is pretty easy.

CLOUDRIPPER

CLOUDRIPPER

BETWEEN THE PINES: BIG PINE

DISTANCE:

20.5-mile loop, counterclockwise

GAIN:
6890 feet

DIFFICULTY:

HIGH POINT: 13,525 ft Cloudripper
LOW POINT: 7750 ft Big Pine Creek Trailhead

PROFILE:

OBJECTIVE: Two peaks
RUNNING: 75%
MODE: Cruiser, Steep, Technical, Adventure, Exposed
SEASON: June–October
PERMIT: No

ACCESS: Big Pine Creek Trailhead
   37°07'31.9"N 118°26'13.4"W
   Pit toilet at parking

APPROACH: From Big Pine, head west on Crocker Avenue, which quickly becomes Glacier Lodge Road. Parking is at the end of the road near Glacier Lodge, about 10 miles outside of town.

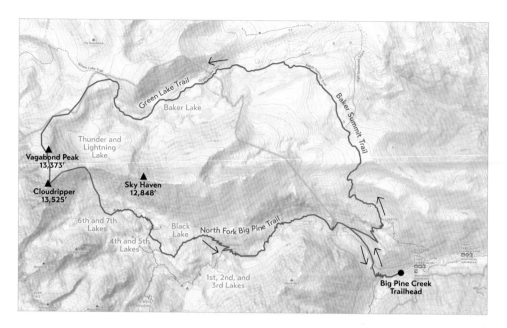

THE ROUTE

Three out of four Sierra trail-running guidebook writers agree — this is the favorite run. It has it all: old-growth trees, remote canyons, two summit scrambles, a long "screeable" descent, and a gentle cruise out on curvy singletrack. All with countless swimming holes along the way.

- Most of the foot traffic starting from Big Pine Creek Trailhead will likely be headed up the Big Pine Creek North Fork Trail. You'll do this, too, for the first mile, before turning onto the less-used Baker Summit Trail. The BST climbs through manzanita and into rough columns of Jeffrey pines before breaking into a high meadow spotted with an assortment of wildflowers.

- The Baker Summit Trail feeds into the Green Lake Trail at an unexpected piece of dirt road, the 32E301, that briefly interrupts your meadow frolic. Now on the Green Lake Trail, you'll head to Baker Lake, where the trail starts to climb more steeply again.

- From the high plateau you'll leave the Green Lake Trail, not dropping to Green Lake but instead picking your way southwest, cross-country, over the low-angle scree to the base of Vagabond Peak (13,374 feet).

- Next, up and over Vagabond and on to Cloudripper — both Class 2. Head up the north flank of Cloudripper, then down the blunt northeast ridge angling toward Sky Haven.

- From the saddle you've got a striking view of Thunder and Lightning Lake down to the north. Take the scree line down the south side of the saddle, and angle toward Sixth Lake where you meet trail again.

- The remaining 7 miles are all downhill. Mostly. Heading to Black Lake from Fourth Lake gives you a better view over Third, Second, and First lakes. But who's counting? You'll feed into the North Fork Trail above First Lake and follow that for the last 3 miles, once again tripping over the enormous pine cones lining the trail.

The Draw It's a well-rounded adventure. You get two valleys, two peaks, all seven of the Numbered Lakes, and the full Sierra spectrum of terrain.

Don't Miss From Cloudripper, check out the Numbered Lakes below. Each one is a different shade of dazzling blue.

Something Extra No. You don't need more. This run has sufficient distance and gain, all in a tidy loop.

Alpine Playground The famous Palisades tower over the Numbered Lakes. This granite crest has five 14ers of its own and the biggest glacier in the Sierra. Temple Crag is right here too, chock-full of long rock-climbing routes.

Cloudripper The second peak is called Cloudripper. Is there any better name for this dark, pointed summit? Then again, with so many bluebird days in the Sierra, there are rarely any clouds for this peak to rip.

In View The Hunchback, Inconsolable Range, Numbered Lakes, the Palisades.

TRAIL BETA

- The spring around 11,060 feet (near the little unnamed lake after Baker Lake) is your last chance to filter enough water to get up and over both peaks and down to the Numbered Lakes. Fill up — going cross-country to two scrambles and a dusty scree descent, you'll be parched.

- Trails near the Numbered Lakes can be busy and may require an annoying (for everyone) amount of weaving through day hikers. Coming down later in the day or doing the loop in the shoulder seasons is a good way to avoid peak-summer crowds.

- Also avoid the Numbered Lakes during the mosquito peak — or run faster to keep the panic-inducing suckers from spoiling an otherwise awesome day.

Kim Strom dropping down to Seventh Lake from the eastern flank of Cloudripper.

BISHOP AREA

MOUNT GOODE

MOUNT GOODE

BISHOP AREA, SOUTH LAKE

DISTANCE:

12.5-mile lollipop, clockwise

GAIN:
4500 feet

DIFFICULTY:

HIGH POINT: 13,085 ft Mount Goode

LOW POINT: 9750 ft Bishop Pass Trailhead, South Lake

PROFILE:

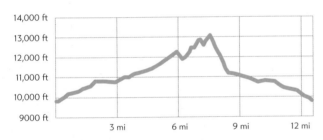

OBJECTIVE: Peak
RUNNING: 65%
MODE: Cruiser, Technical, Adventure
SEASON: June–October
PERMIT: No

ACCESS: Bishop Pass Trailhead, South Lake
    37°10′10.0″N 118°33′57.9″W
    Pit toilet

APPROACH: Head west out of Bishop on Highway 168 (Line Street) to the South Lake turnoff (14.5 miles from 395). Follow South Lake Road to its end.

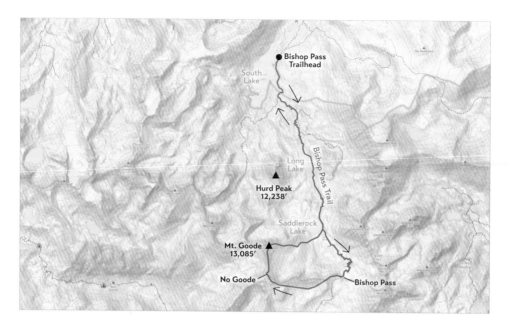

THE ROUTE

Sandwiched between easy miles on a well-established trail, this intro course in Sierra ridge-scrambling takes you from Bishop Pass to the summit of Mount Goode. As with any good ridge adventure, you get to decide when to follow the ridge's crest and when to contour along its flanks. If you're up for the sandy slog and block navigation, you're in for a pretty Goode half-day mountain jaunt. Enough bad Goode puns already — just go run!

- From South Lake, run the wooded trail up a couple of miles and the first thousand feet to the northern tip of Long Lake. Stride along the lake's eastern shore for its length, with great views of Mount Goode. The line you'll be tackling is significantly less steep than the dramatic north face.

- Beyond Long Lake, gradually climb above treeline and past Saddlerock and Bishop lakes before heading up the switchbacks to the top of Bishop Pass.

- Gain the ridge west of Bishop Pass, contouring the southern slope when it makes sense and avoiding ridge-top shenanigans when necessary. This is the start of the cross-country lesson. Pick your way over boulders and slog through DG to the No Goode benchmark (Peak 12,916 ft).

- From No Goode, the ridgeline to Mount Goode looks forbidding, but dropping slightly off the eastern flank makes the continuation to the summit a fun scramble. Class 2.

- Once you're ready to leave the high views behind, make your way down stacked blocks and sandy patches. It's a quick descent on shock-absorbent scree to a use-trail aiming between Bishop and Saddlerock Lakes to rejoin the Bishop Pass Trail.

- Fast and familiar trail back out the way you came in. Linger by the lakes or make a happy dash back to the parking lot.

The Draw A relatively quick lollipop outing that combines excellent trail, a ridge scramble to a summit, and wide backcountry views.

Don't Miss To round out your Bishop experience with a quirky favorite, hit up the Burger Barn on West Line Street on your way back into town.

Something Extra If you're here in the fall, the avenue of aspen near the trailhead will be golden.

Pile Up In November 2017 a large herd of mule deer slid to an icy death down Bishop Pass' north slope. Parts of the macabre remains from the massive 78-deer casualty remained for years along the trail.

Gateway Bishop Pass is another PCT/JMT hiker resupply access. It's also the beginning of the much bigger prize loop through Evolution Basin that finishes over Lamarck Col (page 115).

In View Mount Agassiz, the Palisades, the Citadel, Devils Crags, Le Conte Canyon.

TRAIL BETA

- The trailhead parking and trail can be busy in peak season. Go early for a spot in the lot or run it in the shoulder seasons.

- No Goode bailout. Feel like being done with the run or back to the trailhead sooner? Drop down east from the No Goode benchmark on scree and skip the continuing ridge to Mount Goode.

- **GEAR:** Gaiters to keep the fun descent scree from gathering in a non-fun pile in your shoes.

Navigating a sea of choppy granite above Bishop Pass.

EVOLUTION

EVOLUTION

BISHOP AREA

DISTANCE:

35-mile point-to-point

GAIN:
9040 feet

DESCENT:
9610 feet

DIFFICULTY:
●●●●●

HIGH POINT: 12,880 ft Lamarck Col
LOW POINT: 8760 ft JMT

OBJECTIVE: Three passes
RUNNING: 65%
MODE: Cruiser, Steep, Technical, Adventure
SEASON: June–October typically
PERMIT: No

ACCESS: Bishop Pass Trailhead, South Lake
37°10'10.0"N
118°33'57.9"W
Pit toilet

APPROACH: Head west out of Bishop on Highway 168 (Line Street) to the South Lake turnoff (14.5 miles from 395). Follow South Lake Road to its end.

PROFILE:

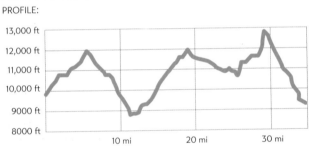

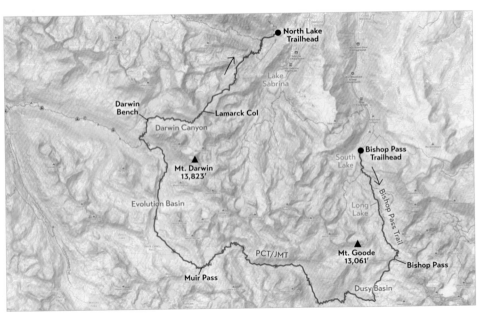

THE ROUTE

Evolution is often the Sierra masterpiece to which all other runs are compared. But first, you should do many other runs to make a fair comparison, and also to be sure you have the experience and fitness to pull this off without winning yourself a Darwin Award. It's high, exhausting, and long — just long enough to really start hurting. It also passes through some of the most cherished and beautiful landscape in the entire Sierra Nevada. So it all evens out.

Starting at South Lake, the route begins with a climb to Bishop Pass. From there, a drop of more than 3000 feet via Dusy Basin takes you to LeConte Canyon. You'll merge onto the John Muir Trail here and start heading north through forest. With a big day already in your legs, begin up the rocky Muir Pass, which takes you back up to 12,000 feet. Descending the pass brings you to the Evolution Basin. Here you'll pass pristine lakes beneath high granite peaks. And through it all, cruiser running.

At the end of the basin, after a short cross-country climb, you'll enter yet another utopia, the Darwin Bench. Once again you're navigating along the shores of several lakes, following on-again off-again trails until you reach the end of the canyon. With a very big day in your legs now, begin the blocky ascent to Lamarck Col. With your back to behemoths mounts Darwin and Mendel, point your shoes down to the Eastside. North Lake, and hopefully a shuttle pick-up, are waiting well over 3000 feet below.

TRAIL BETA

- There are two versions of the Evolution, both share the start and finish at South Lake and North Lake. The difference comes after running through the Evolution Basin. For the homestretch, cross either Lamarck Col (shorter) or Piute Pass (longer).

- South Lake to North Lake via Lamarck Col is the short version, which we feel stays in the most interesting terrain for the entire distance.

- The longer alternative skips the climb to Darwin Bench and continues north from Evolution Basin into Evolution Valley until the Piute Canyon Trail veers off north. That trail leads around and up to Piute Pass before also dropping down to North Lake for a total of 55 miles with 9420 feet of gain.

- Yet another option to consider: Many prefer to go in the opposite direction, North Lake to South Lake.

LAMARCK COL TO PIUTE PASS

LAMARCK COL TO PIUTE PASS

BISHOP AREA, NORTH LAKE

DISTANCE:

17.5-mile loop, clockwise

GAIN:
5380 feet

DIFFICULTY:
●●●●●

HIGH POINT: 12,880 ft Lamarck Col
LOW POINT: 9260 ft North Lake Hiker Parking

PROFILE:

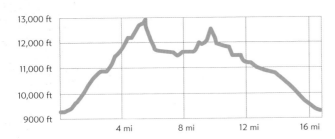

OBJECTIVE: Three Passes
RUNNING: 30%
MODE: Steep, Technical, Adventure, Exposed
SEASON: June–October
PERMIT: No

ACCESS: North Lake Hiker Parking
37°13′50.2″N 118°37′07.4″W
Pit toilet at parking

APPROACH: Take West Line Street (Hwy 168) from Bishop. After Aspendell, turn onto North Lake Road and wind up the dirt road to North Lake. The actual trailhead is a little further up the road, but parking there is reserved for the campground.

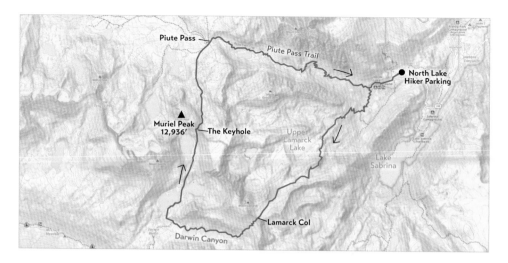

THE ROUTE

Another run for the "Adventure" category. We put this one at a generous 30% runnable, but we're still going to call it a run. Seven miles of slow talus hopping, cross-country navigation, and what may be the only belly-crawl pass in the Sierra, is bookended by two pretty good running trails: to Lamarck Col and down from Piute Pass. It's low-gear running, but high marks for scenery.

- The North Lake parking is probably full since several spokes of trails lead out from here. It's a busy start, but after the first mile or so you might not see anyone else until you're closing the loop. Start up through forest toward Lamarck Lakes and a steady climb to a barren plateau. Follow cairns, but basically head straight up to the visible low spot in the ridge. The final steps to Lamarck Col are steep and potentially hold snow and ice late into summer.

- Dropping from Lamarck, choose your own way to the row of unnamed lakes in Darwin Canyon. Now you get a break from the word "steep" that dominates this run description. Connect the lakes and follow shorelines toward the Darwin Bench. Where the creek bends southwest you'll split to the north, up into the canyon, threading between two lakes. Use your map — this is a tricky section to navigate.

- Aiming toward Muriel Peak at the back of the canyon, keep to the east side of the last lake. Just east of Muriel Peak is the Keyhole, Class 3. You can't see the passage from below, but traverse diagonally toward the north end of the lake until you see the notch. It's a steep, loose slog. The final steps lead you to the Keyhole, where you'll have to prairie-dog yourself through the narrow opening (barely bigger than a thru-hiker's pack) and pop out on the other side.

- Surprise! More talus. And potentially snow or ice on the north-facing slope to start the descent. Again, connect the blue dots, follow the Lost Lakes, picking your way cross-country to Piute Pass, where you might never have been happier to reach a trail.

- Bet you didn't expect to be stumbling around the backcountry quite so long, but it's about to get easier, and faster if you've still got energy. There are another 5 miles between you and the trailhead, but you can switch into autopilot. No more navigating talus. It's finally time to run, and it's all downhill.

The Draw The bulk of the hours spent on the cross-country connector are lonely, long, and humbling.

Don't Miss The Keyhole.

Something Extra Muriel Peak (12,937 feet) is a Class 2-3 scramble along the ridge from the Keyhole, in case you want to check out a summit, too.

Local Lore The Keyhole passes *through* rather than over the Glacier Divide.

Piute Pass The pass was used for trade by Native Americans for thousands of years.

Alone You might see more pikas, bald eagles, marmots, and bear poop than people.

In View Mounts Darwin, Mendel, Humphreys, and Emerson, Piute Crags, Darwin Canyon, lots of lakes.

TRAIL BETA

- Find the Keyhole southeast of Muriel Peak. Tough to spot, but it's the low notch in the ridge.

- Plan to be out longer than you think. Galumphing over talus takes some time.

- GEAR: Bring a headlamp … just in case. Poles, gaiters, and micro spikes can be useful depending on conditions.

Dropping off the west side of Lamarck Col for the long descent of Darwin Canyon.

DRUIDS / WAGANOBE

DRUIDS / WAGANOBE

BISHOP AREA

DISTANCE:

12.5-mile loop, counterclockwise

 GAIN:
3540 feet

DIFFICULTY:

HIGH POINT: **7530 ft**

LOW POINT: **4560 ft**

PROFILE:

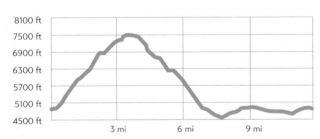

OBJECTIVE: Running
RUNNING: 80%
MODE: Cruiser, Steep
SEASON: Year round
PERMIT: No

ACCESS: Bir Road 37°19'16.0"N 118°26'44.6"W
No facilities

APPROACH: From 395 in Bishop, turn west onto 168 / W Line Street. Make a left onto Barlow Lane. Keep right at the split to Bir Road. Roadside pullout parking is just under 2 miles further.

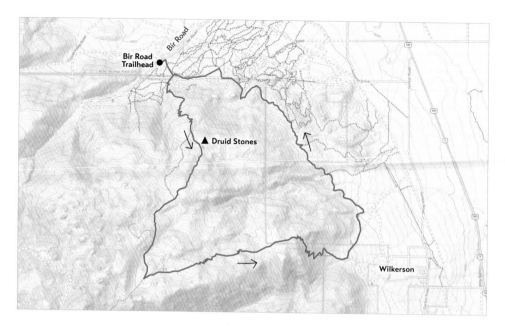

THE ROUTE

This book is full of favorites. If they weren't favorites, you'd be right to assume they wouldn't have made the cut. So, drum roll, this high-desert loop through the Druid Stones, piñon pines, and sagebrush country is another of our tip-top picks. A solid amount of vert, almost a half marathon of miles, and nearly all of it on fantastic DG singletrack. Not too long, not too short, not too tall. Just right.

- Drop off Bir Road and follow the dirt road to the south, working your way to the base of the Druid hillside. Up the switchbacks you go, from sagebrush to open piñons and alongside the magical Druid Stones.

- The trail continues up steeply. With the bulk of the gain behind you, things level out around mile 3.5. Catch the faint fork east in the sagebrush and start to angle down.

- Follow a drainage through rock outcroppings with vibrant green ephedra and the occasional piñon. After a narrow saddle, careen down the series of deep DG switchbacks at carefree high speeds.

- When the trail hits the dirt road, hang a left to start the rolling contour part of the loop. Keep an eye on your map to pick up the singletrack leading northwest along the base of the hillside. Mostly you're following the line that hugs closest to the slope through lumpy foothills on moto and mountain-bike track.

- Keep watching the map to minimize your dirt-road running time and stay on the singletrack network for the final 5 miles back.

The Draw Just the right miles and gain for a sun-drenched singletrack training lap in the best of Bishop's sage, boulders, and piñons.

Don't Miss The Druid Stones. They look impressive from a distance and even more so up close, especially when you explore their maze-like corridors. While not nearly as famous among climbers as the nearby Buttermilks, they are the same type of rock, but the 1200-foot approach keeps the crowds away.

Something Extra For a shorter version, run the locals' favorite starting from Bir Road. This condensed 5-mile and 2050-foot climb, Druid Loop, heads straight up past the big granite stones, then loops right back down (at about 6900 feet), all on buffed singletrack through the sage.

Farm Fresh Organics As you curve past the community of Wilkerson, you're right above Apple Hill Ranch. Make a mental marker to visit this local farm for your stock-up on organics: delicious fruits and veggies, honey and preserves, and a free-range egg box at their gate.

Mountain Rambler For local craft beer and good grub, stop by the Mountain Rambler Brewery on South Main Street in Bishop.

Soak It Up Geothermal activity in the Owens Valley is the source of numerous hot springs. These waters have been visited for their healing properties since before recorded history. Take your towel and trunks to nearby Keough's Hot Springs to recuperate from run-accumulated aches.

In View White Mountains, Inyo Mountains, Owens Valley, Mount Tom, Wheeler Crest.

TRAIL BETA

- You will be scuffing along unofficial trails; this is a good place to use your map and GPX track.

- No water. Bring plenty.

- This one's extra special in the winter months or early summer mornings. Otherwise, expect it to get hot.

Winter conditions on the Druids Trail.

BISHOP CANAL

BISHOP CANAL

BISHOP

DISTANCE:

3-mile loop, clockwise

GAIN:
Flat

DIFFICULTY:
●○○○○

HIGH POINT: 4150 ft
LOW POINT: 4110 ft

PROFILE:

East Line St.

Bishop Creek Canal

OBJECTIVE: Running
RUNNING: 100%
MODE: Cruiser
SEASON: Year round
PERMIT: No

ACCESS: E Line Street
37°21'41.1"N
118°23'09.3"W
No facilities

APPROACH: From the center of Bishop, turn east on E Line Street. Parking is in a gravel lot beside the canal at the edge of town.

THE ROUTE

On that rare, rainy rest day, or when you just want to put in a minimum amount of movement, the Lazy Loop along the Bishop Canal is the local way to go. Sip one final cup of Black Sheep coffee and mosey over to the east end of town. The canal is a popular area for runners, walkers, fishermen, and grazing cows. Set between water and sage and beneath cottonwoods, the views to the Sierra and the White Mountains on either side are more than worth breaking a sweat. Do a quick loop and head into Sage to Summit to boulder away the afternoon.

TRAIL BETA

While you're here, you can wander off on any of the side roads to run longer.

TUNGSTEN PEAK

TUNGSTEN PEAK

BISHOP AREA

DISTANCE:

5.5-mile lollipop, clockwise

GAIN:
1950 feet

DIFFICULTY:
●○○○○

HIGH POINT: 5950 ft Tungsten Peak
LOW POINT: 4660 ft Tungsten Peak Trailhead

PROFILE:

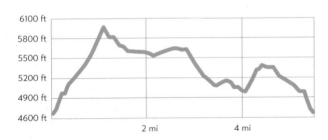

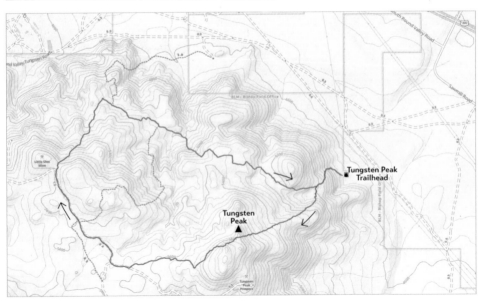

OBJECTIVE: Peak
RUNNING: 75%
MODE: Cruiser, Steep
SEASON: Year round
PERMIT: No

ACCESS: Tungsten Peak TH
  37°22'31.4"N
  118°30'51.8"W
  No facilities

TRAIL BETA

It's so much fun you might consider another lap, or make it your go-to training hill.

APPROACH: From 395, north of Bishop, take Sawmill Road west of the highway. Past the paved South Round Valley Road, take the first right turn onto a dirt road following the power lines. After about a mile the road splits. Go left and then make a quick right up to the Tungsten Peak Trailhead parking.

THE ROUTE

Tungsten Peak doesn't look like much considering the High Sierra just beyond, but the rocky top is a great lookout point and the running trails around this little peak are some of the best in the Owens Valley. The route follows a mix of trails. Worn in by a variety of users, the hiking trails, dirt roads, and dirt-bike tracks are generally easy to follow, but constantly change depending on use. As you weave through sage and boulder towers, this is another track where it helps to pay attention to your map.

TUNGSTEN HILLS

TUNGSTEN HILLS

BISHOP AREA

DISTANCE:

11-mile loop, counterclockwise

 GAIN:
2100 feet

DIFFICULTY:

HIGH POINT: 6130 ft
LOW POINT: 4590 ft

PROFILE:

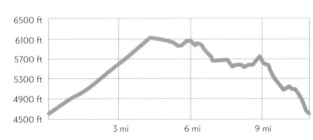

OBJECTIVE: Running
RUNNING: 100%
MODE: Cruiser
SEASON: Year round
PERMIT: No

ACCESS: Round Valley Tungsten Road
37°23'15.0"N 118°32'47.8"W
No facilities

APPROACH: From Highway 395, 5 miles north of Bishop, turn southwest onto Sawmill Road followed by a quick right onto South Round Valley Road. Stay on S Round Valley Road for 2 miles, then turn left onto the dirt Round Valley Tungsten Road. Half a mile down, park at a turn out near the foot of the Tungsten Hills.

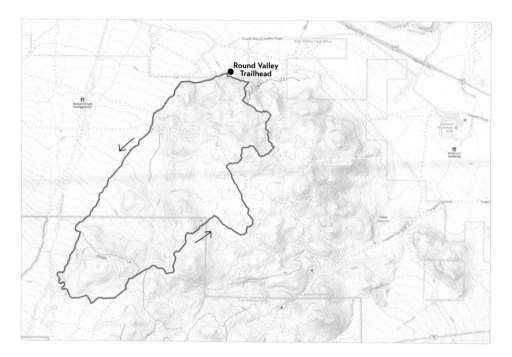

THE ROUTE

The Tungsten Hills are chock full of interweaving singletrack and dirt roads that face you toward the big peaks and then swing you round for views over the Owens Valley. This nearly half-marathon loop creeps into Buttermilk Country at the foot of the Bishop skyline. With fast-flowing dirt and close proximity to town, it's little wonder these hills have been the chosen site of Bishop's ultra races for years.

- Go west up the dirt road hugging the base of the Tungsten Hills and aim yourself toward Mount Tom. Keep your map handy when side roads beckon. With width to run side-by-side with friends, you'll still need to pay attention to navigate all the road splits.

- So far it's been a straight shot, but now the route starts a series of twists and turns until you get close to the 6-mile mark. Soon you're on singletrack and arcing north around one of Tungsten's higher mounds, higher in fact than Tungsten Peak.

- When the singletrack again hits dirt road at about 7.5 miles, wind north and keep left when the road comes to a fork. From here, it's another half mile before you turn right, cross the road, and hop onto singletrack for the remainder of the run.

- Now it's nothing but aggressive running and quick pedaling over bumpy rolls until you reach one last drop to, *Whoa, the car.*

The Draw Half-marathon training with gorgeous views of the skyline that features just about everything that great about Bishop. Run it all winter or early on a scorching hot day.

Don't Miss The Buttermilks. These world famous (among climbers) granite boulders are just beyond the southernmost tip of this run. With a few extra miles you can make a detour to see what all the fuss is about. In the winter months, the huge quartz-monzonite blocks are abuzz with boulderers clustered around in groups, grunting their way up to tiny summits.

Something Extra Tungsten Peak. With a 1.5 mile, 340-foot side trip you can take in the namesake summit. This peak is also featured in one of our shorter runs, a 5-mile loop with a hearty vert-to-miles ratio (page 139).

Local Lore The Tungsten Hills were extensively mined in the first half of the 1900s. Tungsten, AKA Wolfram, still has many applications and is noteworthy for having the highest melting point and highest tensile strength of known elements. Rockhounds like to wander these hills hunting red garnets and quartz crystals common to the ore-bearing rocks.

Millpond Nearby Millpond Recreation Area is a friendly park setting with a big pond, open lawn, and shade trees. It's also the starting point for ultra races that go through the Tungsten Hills and Buttermilk Country. Each fall, it hosts the Millpond Music Festival.

In View Mount Tom, Wheeler Crest, Basin Mountain, Mount Humphreys, the Buttermilks, White Mountains, Owens Valley.

TRAIL BETA

- Follow your map. Follow your map. Then, follow your map. There are lots of roads and trails to get lost on. Or, leave your map behind and get lost for a day of exploration.

- No water — bring all you need.

Kim Strom happily hurdling sage.

GRANITE PARK

GRANITE PARK

BISHOP AREA , PINE CREEK

DISTANCE:

←——————→

21-mile out-and-back

GAIN:
7040 feet

DIFFICULTY:
●●●●○

HIGH POINT: **13,206 ft Mount Julius Caesar**
LOW POINT: **7400 ft Pine Creek Trailhead**

PROFILE:

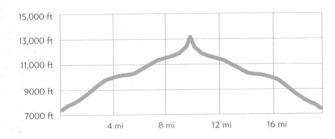

OBJECTIVE: Peak
RUNNING: 60%
MODE: Technical, Adventure, Exposed
SEASON: July–October typically
PERMIT: No

ACCESS: Pine Creek Trailhead
37°21'41.1"N 118°41'28.2"W
No facilities

APPROACH: 12 miles north of Bishop, drive west to the end of
Pine Creek Canyon Road.

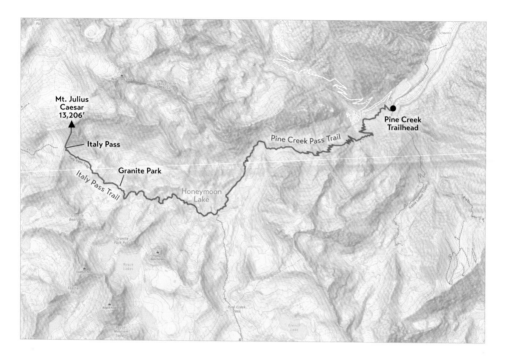

THE ROUTE

Veni, vidi ... Yet again, it takes some distance to get to the really good stuff in the Sierra. The 21-mile out-and-back to Mount Julius Caesar takes you through the extraordinary Granite Park to a remote summit scramble overlooking endless gray rock. Friends, Romans, countrymen, there are no shortage of swim stops along the way to soak your sweaty self on a hot day. Did you catch the reference?

- From Pine Creek Trailhead, the route starts by passing through the Pine Creek Pack Station to an old mining road. Don't head the opposite way — that's Gable Lakes Trail. The climb starts in the forest, with some shade for both the start and finish. Honeymoon Lake comes 6 miles into the run just after the trail splits from Pine Creek Pass Trail.

- After Honeymoon Lake, the trail is unfrequented and unmaintained, but not un-awesome. It winds through more shaded forest until reaching the open meadows and tall spires of Granite Park. The valley leads straight to Italy Pass. The route is marked with cairns, but rock piles sitting on rocks aren't always easy to see — just piece together the worn trail sections and aim for the obvious low pass.

- From Italy Pass, it's an 800-foot scramble to Mount Julius Caesar. Beware the first highpoint; the second is the summit. On the way up, keep on the ridgeline for solid boulder hopping.

- Note the sandy, southwest-leading gully at the saddle between the double summits for a quicker descent on mostly loose gravel back to Italy Pass.

- Reverse it back through Granite Park, past all the lakes and streams. It almost always goes faster going back down, unless you stop for another dip. No rush to leave this quiet haven.

The Draw Summit views! Plenty of lakes for swimming and streams to fill bottles.

Don't Miss Look down to Italy Lake from the summit ... it's shaped like a boot ... sorta.

Something Extra Make it an even bigger day with a beeline from Granite Park to Granite Park Pass. All cross-country, funnel between Royce Lakes and Treasure Benchmark, working toward Pine Creek Pass. From the pass, mellow trail wraps around to loop back to Honeymoon Lake.

Mine in the Sky The Pine Creek Mine was the last operational Tungsten Mine in the US. It closed in 1990 and is now inhabited by bighorn sheep.

In View Bear Creek Spire, Peppermint Peak, Italy Lake, Granite Park, Mount Gabb, Mount Dade, Feather Peak, Royce Peak, Mount Abbot, Mount Tom.

TRAIL BETA

- After Honeymoon Lake, the trail is not officially maintained. Follow the use-trail and cairns up to Italy Pass.

- From Italy Pass to the summit, it's a fun scramble if you stay on the south ridge. Class 2-3 on good rock.

Passing Italy Pass and about to go into 4WD for the summit of Julius Caesar.

TABLELANDS

TABLELANDS

BISHOP AREA, TABLELANDS, PLEASANT VALLEY

DISTANCE:

7.5-mile loop, clockwise

GAIN:
830 feet

DIFFICULTY:
●○○○○

HIGH POINT: **4880 ft**
LOW POINT: **4300 ft**

PROFILE:

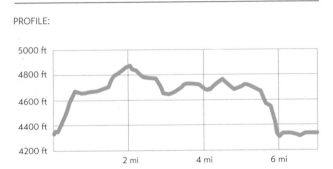

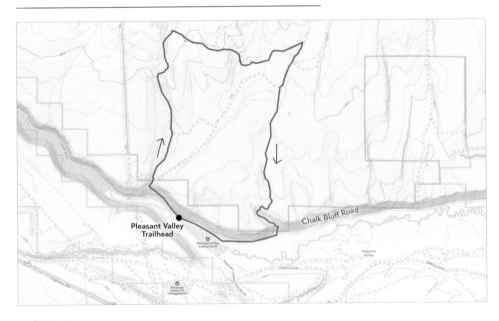

OBJECTIVE: Running
RUNNING: 100%
MODE: Cruiser
SEASON: Year round
PERMIT: No

ACCESS: Pleasant Valley
37°24'38.3"N
118°30'39.9"W
Pit toilets at Pleasant
Valley Campground

APPROACH: From Highway
395, turn northeast
onto Pleasant Valley
Dam Road, 5 miles north
of Bishop. Park at the
turnout 2 miles up the
road where it intersects
with Chalk Bluff Road.

THE ROUTE

Starting from Pleasant Valley, the run is a mellow loop mostly on dirt roads. With far-flung views across the Owens Valley with the Whites and the Sierra on either side, the first 6 miles mostly roll along a tire-worn doubletrack. The ground beneath your feet changes colors from gray to gold to purple before running out, unexpectedly, above a rocky rim. Dropping in puts you among a maze of otherworldly boulders. Your so-far steady pace comes to a halt for the fun of exploring.

The loop takes you onto the Volcanic Tablelands, which were formed by an eruption of the Long Valley Caldera about 700,000 years ago. The wild desert area is known for the petroglyphs spread throughout. You'll have to find these by exploring on your own, as they're better preserved by not broadcasting their locations.

TRAIL BETA

Best done on days that aren't 100 degrees, or plan on taking a plunge in the Owens River for a cool-down.

MOUNT STARR

MOUNT STARR

BISHOP AREA, ROCK CREEK

DISTANCE:

←——————→

8.5-mile out-and-back

GAIN:
2800 feet

DIFFICULTY:
●●○○○

HIGH POINT: 12,840 ft Mount Starr
LOW POINT: 10,260 ft Little Lakes Valley Trailhead

PROFILE:

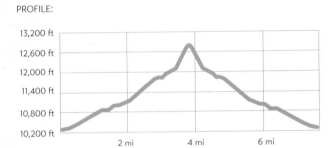

OBJECTIVE: Peak
RUNNING: 75%
MODE: Cruiser, Technical
SEASON: June–October
PERMIT: No

ACCESS: Little Lakes Valley Trailhead
   37°26'06.9"N 118°44'49.9"W
   Pit toilet, campground

APPROACH: From Highway 395, head west on Rock Creek Road
   at Tom's Place. Parking is at the end of Rock Creek Road.

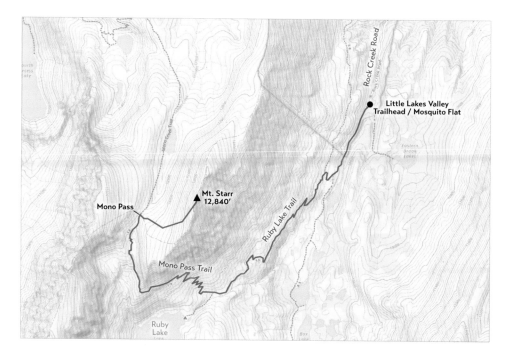

THE ROUTE

If you're new to Sierra trail running, this is a mini version of a bigger peak run. Never too hard and not at all too long, the out-and-back to Mount Starr serves up a little of everything: forest trail, alpine, talus, scree, and a summit ridge. Use it as an ideal check for your comfort level in typical Sierra terrain before moving on to the bigger runs with a *lot* of everything.

- Start up the popular Little Lakes Valley Trail. After a half mile, turn west on the Ruby Lake Trail. Zig and zag your way up gently rising DG until the trail junction for Ruby Lake.

- At the split, stay right and head up the Mono Pass Trail, climbing numerous switchbacks to Mono Pass, a wide-open and barren landscape.

- From the pass, a use-trail leads to the west flank of Mount Starr. Follow the trail as best as you can, seeking solid ground and always aiming for the ridgeline. The higher you get, the easier it is to move on the talus and scree. Once on the ridge, easy boulder hopping leads over several false summits to the ridge's highpoint.

- From the summit of Mount Starr, looking down reveals the best track. Take your pick — ski the scree or hop down boulders. Either way, you'll quickly return to Mono Pass for a smooth, cushy run all the way to the car.

The Draw Starting at one of the higher Sierra trailheads allows easy access to a classic High Sierra landscape, getting you above treeline for an alpine appetizer without too much effort.

Don't Miss The half-mile round-trip detour to Ruby Lake provides a scenic lunch and swim spot.

Something Extra Start down canyon to make it a little longer. Park at Rock Creek Lake, run along the west shore, and follow the trail to Rock Creek Lake Campground where it turns south to head up the canyon and eventually meet the paved road before Little Lakes Valley Trailhead and Mosquito Flat. This adds an extra 5 miles and 700 feet of vertical.

Mosquito Flat Note the name. This valley is infamous for mosquitos. Unless you want to do speed work outrunning these tiny monsters, go outside of peak mosquito season.

Glacial Trough The Little Lakes Basin that you'll look down on from the Mono Pass Trail is a classic glacier-carved U-shaped valley now filled with lakes.

Going, Going, Gong For the trail runners who also rock climb, Rock Creek Canyon's Gong Show Wall is a premier granite climbing destination for both sport and trad routes. The summer sequence is to run in the morning, climb in the afternoon. Use the *Mammoth Area Rock Climbs* guidebook by Marty Lewis.

In View Little Lakes Valley, Bear Creek Spire, mounts Mills, Abbot, and Dade.

TRAIL BETA

- Get to the trailhead early — the Little Lakes Valley Parking fills fast. If it is full, you'll have to find a roadside pullout without a No Parking sign.

Dan Patitucci on the final approach to the summit of Mount Starr.

LOWER ROCK CREEK

LOWER ROCK CREEK

BISHOP AREA, ROCK CREEK

DISTANCE:

15.5-mile out-and-back

GAIN:
2250 feet

DIFFICULTY:
●●○○○

HIGH POINT: 6900 ft Rock Creek Road
LOW POINT: 4980 ft Lower Rock Creek Trailhead

PROFILE:

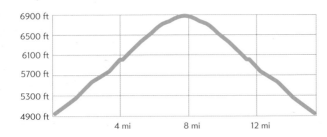

OBJECTIVE: Canyon
RUNNING: 100%
MODE: Cruiser
SEASON: Year round
PERMIT: No

ACCESS: Lower Rock Creek Trailhead
37°28'48.9"N 118°36'13.4"W
Porta-pot

APPROACH: From 395, exit west onto Gorge Road and make a quick right onto Old Sherwin Grade/Lower Rock Creek Road. In 3 miles, you reach Paradise. The Lower Rock Creek Trailhead parking is just after the creek crossing.

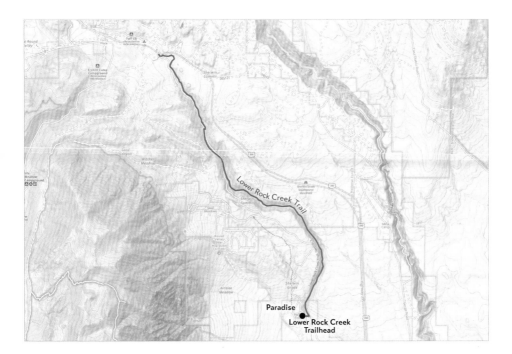

THE ROUTE

This gem of a hidden canyon is a trail runner's paradise. As it turns out, Paradise is also the name of the small community where your run begins. Following the Sherwin Grade, the slope rising from Bishop to Mammoth, the trail is a quick-access option with plenty of shade, rushing water, and a runnable gradient. Buffed singletrack at the base of the big mountains makes this a go-to run any time of year.

- From the Lower Rock Creek Trailhead, the trail initially skirts private property, tunnels under a lush birch canopy, and criss-crosses its way up the lively Rock Creek over a series of bridges.

- A few miles in, the canyon narrows and the trail becomes rockier. Weaving among the boulders, drop into a shaded flat under a tall stand of Jeffrey pines. Keep your eyes peeled for foot-soak spots along the river — useful on the way back down. Soon you'll cross Lower Rock Creek Road for the first time.

- Another mile of curving singletrack brings you to a second road crossing. Take a sharp right, cross a bridge on the road, and pick up the trail on the opposite side.

- This last section is especially spectacular in the fall when the aspens are at their peak gold. Steady, low-angle turns up Whisky Canyon bring you to the upper trailhead where Lower Rock Creek Road meets Highway 395 near the top of the Sherwin Grade.

- It's time to turn around and quickly undo 2250 feet of gain. Run your way back down through paradise to Paradise. Be sure not to miss the canyon-framed views of Mount Tom and the Wheeler Crest as you near the trail's southern exit.

The Draw Year-round running: winter sun, spring flowers, summer shade, golden autumn aspen.

Don't Miss Masonry bark of the tall Jeffrey pines.

Caldera Lower Rock Creek Canyon is carved into the Sherwin Grade that separates the lower, hotter, Owens Valley from the higher, cooler Long Valley Caldera, one of the world's largest calderas.

Deep Ruts Mule teams pulling heavy wagon loads carved deep ruts of old-West history into the volcanic tuff. Remnants of these 19th-century wagon roads along the Sherwin Grade have more recently become favorite tracks for mountain bikers.

Birders Listen for the cascading trill of the canyon wren, or sharp alerts of nesting peregrines. Great horned owls also nest nearby.

In View Mount Tom.

TRAIL BETA

- This trail is also a favorite for mountain bikers, so keep an attentive ear and eye out rounding the bends.

- Choose your distance. Park on either end of the trail. Go up first, down first, turn around when you want.

Deep in Lower Rock Creek Canyon.

MAMMOTH AREA

MOUNT BALDWIN

MOUNT BALDWIN

MAMMOTH AREA

DISTANCE:

15-mile out-and-back

GAIN:
5310 feet

DIFFICULTY:

●●●○○

HIGH POINT: **12,614 ft Mount Baldwin**
LOW POINT: **7620 ft Convict Lake**

PROFILE:

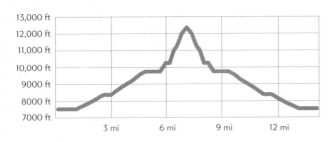

OBJECTIVE: Peak
RUNNING: 60%
MODE: Steep, Adventure, Technical, Exposed
SEASON: July–October
PERMIT: No

ACCESS: Convict Lake Trailhead
  37°35'21.2"N 118°51'15.7"W
  Toilet, water

APPROACH: From Hwy 395, take Convict Lake Road. Keep left around the southeast shore of Convict Lake. Trailhead parking is at the end of the road.

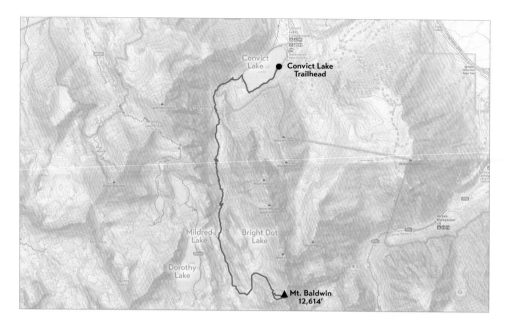

THE ROUTE

A sharp summit, pastel peaks, improbable forms, crystals galore ... this hallucinogenic tour with chocolate-brown cliffs and swirly-twirly marble is not your typical Eastside view. If for some unexplainable reason you don't already love the Sierra, Mount Baldwin might just win you over.

• From the Convict Lake Trailhead, follow the southern shoreline until it joins the main trail to head up Convict Canyon. In and out of tree cover, the trail winds its way south through the rugged, steep-sided canyon until you emerge at Mildred Lake into wide and level grassy meadows.

• Break from the main path that leads to Lake Dorothy, continuing south on a faint, swampy trail until a small creek from Mount Baldwin cues your climb eastward. Watch for cairns that mark the way through initially thick brush to a barren plateau. From here the trail becomes more obvious and ascends northward below Baldwin's western aspect.

• The climb gets steeper, dropping Bright Dot Lake to a shrinking dot below as your ascent angles up the northwest ridge. A short scramble through a steep band pops you out in a dazzling patch of calcite crystals. Two-steps-forward, one-slide-back your way up the loose western slope to the summit. Class 2-3.

• There's none of the usual granite here. Check out the views along the ridge northward toward Mount Morrison and, in the opposite direction, wild ribbons of red, orange, and white rock. You have a full panorama to Red Slate Mountain, Lake Dorothy, and the steep drops into McGee Canyon.

• That two-steps-forward, one-slide-back on the uphill is now a continuously playful downhill as you start back down and out.

The Draw Wildly colorful, with a trail (although sometimes faint) all the way to the summit.

Don't Miss The Restaurant at Convict Lake is a local favorite for fine dining in the Eastern Sierra. Might want to change your sweaty shirt first.

Something Extra If you like lakes and flatter running, finish along the northwest shore of Convict Lake to see the full lake loop.

Local Lore The contorted rock of this zone is called roof-pendant. It's composed of previously sedimentary strata that were metamorphosed into marble, slate, and quartzite by heat and pressure from the intrusion of more geologically recent granite.

Convicts The lake called Wit-sa-nap by the Paiute was believed to provide special refuge for mountain fish and spirit legend. In 1871, settlers renamed this peaceful haven Convict Lake after a band of criminals escaped from prison in Carson City, Nevada. They were tracked to the lake by a pursuing posse and all hell broke loose in a shootout that cost life and limb on both sides.

In View Mount Morrison, Red Slate Mountain, Lake Dorothy, the Minarets, Long Valley Caldera, Glass Mountains.

TRAIL BETA

- Wait for snowmelt and runoff to lessen and make creek crossings easier and safer. Consider wading through without taking off your shoes.

- GEAR: Poles are useful in the loose terrain and for the creek crossings.

Churning along through a chocolatey layer to the summit of Mount Baldwin.

DEER LAKES

DEER LAKES

MAMMOTH AREA

DISTANCE:

13-mile loop, clockwise

GAIN:
3390 feet

DIFFICULTY:

HIGH POINT: 11,210 ft

LOW POINT: 9025 ft Lake George Picnic Area

PROFILE:

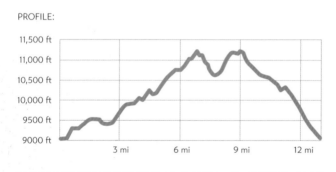

OBJECTIVE: Pass
RUNNING: 90%
MODE: Cruiser
SEASON: June–October
PERMIT: No

ACCESS: Crystal Lake Trailhead / Lake George Picnic Area
37°36'10.8"N 119°00'37.6"W
Pit toilets

APPROACH: From Main Street / Hwy 203, continue straight as the road turns into Lake Mary Road and follow this up into the Mammoth Lakes Basin. Just past Lake Mary, turn left onto Around Lake Mary Road, then right on Lake George Road up to the trailhead parking lot.

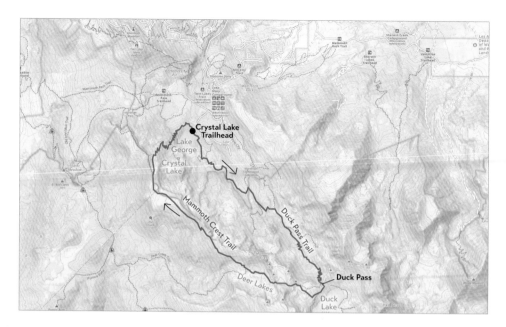

THE ROUTE

If you take the *running* part of trail running seriously, this one's for you. For the rest of us, no matter how hard you try, there are few excuses not to run. This little race track above Mammoth Lakes is a Mammoth Running Club favorite and is one of the few runs in this book where you may see an Olympian.

- Follow the lakeside path around the eastern shore and across the outlet of Lake George. The trail climbs through the pine forest past Lake Barrett.

- Just over 2 miles in, turn right onto the Emerald Lake Trail to meet up with the Duck Pass Trail. More wooded terrain and a string of glittering lakes lead up and over Duck Pass.

- Just beyond the pass, keep right at the fork. You only get a few level strides along the trail contouring above Duck Lake. In less than a quarter mile, leave the main trail, angling upslope on a fainter track. Follow this for about a mile before merging onto the Mammoth Crest Trail.

- The Mammoth Crest Trail dips down into Deer Lakes Basin on the backside of the crest. Just past Deer Lakes keep right, regaining the crest before starting a speedy downward glide.

- After a long stretch of fifth-gear cruising through a wide-open expanse of DG, the Mammoth Crest Trail drops to the right directly above Crystal Lake. A squiggle of switchbacks through the woods closes the loop.

The Draw Great as a trail-running intro with easy navigating practice and altitude training.

Don't Miss If you run up an appetite for tacos, Salsa's Taqueria on Old Mammoth Road is the place for Mexican takeout or chowing down right then and there.

Something Extra Cool off in one of the lakes along the way, or plop into Lake George at the end of the miles.

Mammoth Track Club Olympian and longtime holder of the American marathon record, Deena Kastor, and other elite-caliber athletes have called Mammoth Lakes home and trained on these trails. Andrew Kastor is the head coach of Mammoth Track Club, the local running club and an elite training group. Since its founding in 2001, the club has cultivated 14 Olympians and 64 National Champions, and set 29 American records.

Crystal Crag The monolith landmark feature above Lake George is named for a beautiful and unusually thick band of quartz high on its north arête. The granite tower is well known for its classic climbing routes.

Provisions Most anything you need is available in the corner shopping center (Old Mammoth Road and Meridian Blvd), from groceries, to matinees with popcorn, to print-bound books from the Booky Joint.

In View The Minarets, Mount Ritter and Banner Peak, Mammoth Mountain, Crystal Crag.

TRAIL BETA

- Duck Pass is a popular hike. Especially during high season, be prepared to share this portion of the trail.

Fast and clean DG running.

MAMMOTH ROCK

MAMMOTH ROCK

MAMMOTH AREA

DISTANCE:

7-mile loop, clockwise

GAIN:
1230 feet

DIFFICULTY:
●○○○○

HIGH POINT: 8480 ft Old Mammoth Road
LOW POINT: 7860 ft Mammoth Rock Trailhead

PROFILE:

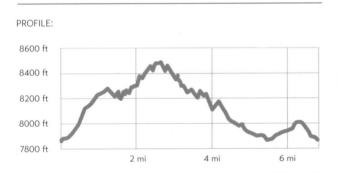

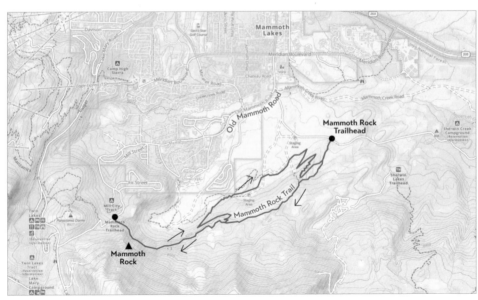

OBJECTIVE: Running
RUNNING: 100%
MODE: Cruiser
SEASON: 3 season
PERMIT: No

ACCESS: Mammoth Rock Trail
37°37'44.2"N
118°57'25.3"W
No facilities

TRAIL BETA

The north-facing slope will hold snow in winter and offers better running in the other seasons.

APPROACH: From Highway 395, take the exit for Hwy 203 and Mammoth Lakes. After 2 miles on Hwy 203, turn left onto Meridian Blvd, left onto Old Mammoth Road, and one more left onto Sherwin Creek Road to pass through town. Parking is a mile down, just past the trailhead.

THE ROUTE

Close to the mountains but not fully in them, this Mammoth locals' favorite is perfect for a quick escape on flowy singletrack. Trail running for runners, and at the ideal altitude for training, this low-angle trail leads from sand and sagebrush into the forest to Mammoth Rock beneath Mammoth Mountain. After a visit to the iconic marble and limestone pillar, the return trip meanders through Sherwin Meadows along lengthy switchbacks. Great for beginner trailers and good enough to repeat for not-so-off-the-beaten-track training. Heads up for mountain bikes on this one!

MINARETS

MINARETS

MAMMOTH AREA

DISTANCE:

21-mile lollipop, clockwise

GAIN:
4600 feet

DIFFICULTY:

● ● ● ○ ○

HIGH POINT: **10,317 ft Cecile Lake**
LOW POINT: **7560 ft Devils Postpile Ranger Station**

PROFILE:

OBJECTIVE: Lakes
RUNNING: 80%
MODE: Cruiser, Technical
SEASON: June–October
PERMIT: No

ACCESS: Devils Postpile Ranger Station
37°37′48.0″N 119°05′04.8″W
Toilets, water

APPROACH: From Highway 395, drive 10 miles west on Minaret Road (S.R. 203) to Minaret Vista. Park at the Mammoth Mountain Ski Area and take the shuttle bus for the final 8 miles along the narrow mountain road. The bus runs mid-June through early September and is mandatory unless you arrive outside its daily or seasonal operating hours. Check the NPS site for current schedule and cost.

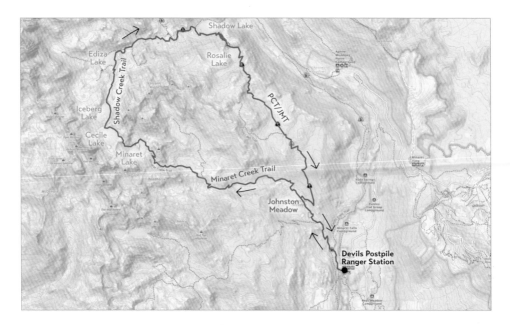

THE ROUTE

This isn't the high desert, there's no sage or squelching heat. The Minarets have a decidedly different look and feel from the rest of the Sierra. Outside Mammoth, a spiky skyline towers above lush, flower-filled meadows, shaded forest, and abundant lakes. Through it all is a flowing trail that lets you take in the views while running fast.

- Follow the Devils Postpile trail south, just for a quarter mile, before veering right over a bridge to the Minaret Lake Trailhead. Two miles in the woods climb to Johnston Meadow. Continue along Minaret Creek toward its source.

- From the far side of Minaret Lake, follow the faint trail through talus and up a rocky step to gain a bench overlooking Cecile Lake, the highpoint of the loop. Traverse above the eastern shore, picking your way across the rocks toward the north end of Cecile Lake.

- Descend a steep, loose slope toward Iceberg Lake, again angling down above the east side of the lake to rejoin smoother trail.

- Resume easy running on the gentle downhill of the Shadow Creek Trail.

Here you'll encounter more day hikers and backpackers as you descend through tiered alpine meadows, past Ediza Lake with its views of Ritter and Banner, then back into the trees along Shadow Creek.

- Pick up the JMT before you reach Shadow Lake and prepare for the final climb of the day. The rise through the woods could probably be gained in about a dozen high-steps straight up, but with nearly flat hairpin turns you'll be running a much longer, low-angle, distance. Passing Rosalie and Gladys lakes brings you to the start of your descent.

- Fast running on a tidy trail through the woods drops you back to Johnston Meadow. Retrace the final miles to the trailhead for a foot-soak in the Middle Fork of the San Joaquin River.

The Draw High points for smooth running in the trees and stumble-worthy views on the slower-moving high section.

Don't Miss Find a spot for lunch near Minaret Lake, especially idyllic with an hourglass-shaped shoreline, wildflowers, and healthy hemlocks.

Something Extra Devils Postpile. You're already this close, so take the half mile cool-down saunter to visit the columnar basalt rock formation that the National Monument is famous for.

Rainbow Falls If you still have it in you, 2 miles down-river is another attraction of the area: a waterfall in the San Joaquin River known to cast a rainbow in its mist at midday.

In View Clyde Minaret, Ritter and Banner, lots of lakes.

TRAIL BETA

- The shuttle to the trailhead reduces emissions and congestion. Be sure to check the NPS schedule and don't miss the last bus out. Holidays and weekends can be busy. Reservations recommended.

- If you arrive outside of shuttle operating hours or dates, you must pay an amenity fee at the Minaret Vista Station.

- Keep your map handy to navigate intersections and stay on route.

- Check snow conditions for the Minarets at the ranger station. The north-facing descent from Cecile Lake to Iceberg can hold snow late into the season.

- During peak mosquito season, consider one of those high-desert trails instead.

Passing Iceberg Lake before the drop to Ediza Lake.

GARNET LAKE

GARNET LAKE

MAMMOTH AREA

DISTANCE:

20-mile lollipop, clockwise

 GAIN:
6470 feet

DIFFICULTY:

HIGH POINT: **10,170 ft**

LOW POINT: **7200 ft Rush Creek Trailhead**

PROFILE:

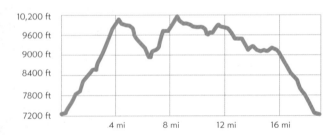

OBJECTIVE: Lake
RUNNING: 75%
MODE: Cruiser
SEASON: June–October
PERMIT: No

ACCESS: Rush Creek Trailhead
    37°46′49.5″N 119°07′41.7″W
    Flush toilet at trailhead

APPROACH: From Hwy 395, follow the June Lake Loop (Hwy
    158) to the north end of Silver Lake. Parking is near the
    Silver Lake Campground and pack station.

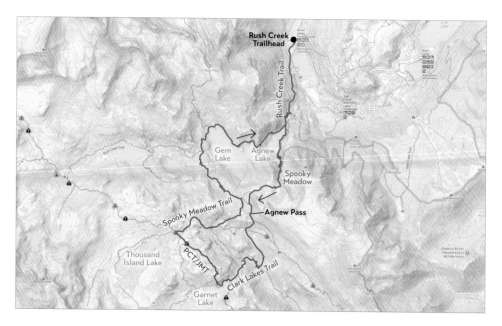

THE ROUTE

Time on feet. That's what this long run is good for. It's easy to get lost in thought, and geography, in the disorienting forested miles. Losing sense of time and place and plodding along, suddenly you've just slipped into the ultra-shuffle mindset.

- Take the Rush Creek Trail, angling south above Silver Lake. The first 3.5 miles (which are also the final 3.5 miles) start up gradually, leading to tighter switchbacks, rocky steps, and crossing over the old tram line to the hydroelectric plants.

- Before Agnew Lake, split to Spooky Meadow Trail around the east side of the lake and climb switchbacks up to Spooky Meadow. Before Clark Lake and just after a small lake, hang a left on a worn grassy path, the cutoff trail, to reach Agnew Pass. Now on Clark Lakes Trail, you're headed downhill to intercept River Trail. Don't get into too much of a groove following River Trail — you're on it less than a mile before the unmarked cutoff trail to Garnet Lake.

- The trail takes some attention to follow as it leads uphill to the lake. The view across Garnet Lake to Ritter and

Banner is definitely the highlight of the run. Enjoy one of the Sierra's iconic viewpoints before heading back into the trees.

- You may have noticed all the signposts have directed toward Thousand Island Lake. Now, you're finally headed in that direction via Ruby and Emerald lakes first. After Thousand Island Lake, a stretch of PCT winds over to the Spooky Meadow Trail and the northern tip of Clark Lake — the narrow waist of the figure-eight.

- From there, flowing miles of forest running lead to the north point of Gem Lake and above its northern shore on the Rush Creek Trail. The familiar view overlooking Agnew Lake is a relief when you reach the dam and can see the switchbacks from much earlier in this journey. It's finally all downhill, reconnecting with the way it all started.

The Draw A big up, then miles of shaded forest running perfect for hot summer days.

Don't Miss A few hard-to-find unmarked turns.

Something Extra Dropped off next to the June Lake Fire Station is an 18-foot-tall glacial erratic, Balanced Rock. This giant boulder was carried to its perch by the Rush Creek Glacier and has become a roadside attraction.

B - double E - double R - U - N Since 1932, the Tiger Bar in June Lake holds one of California's oldest liquor licenses. Drink up there or visit June Lake Brewing for post-run hydration.

Dam and Tram The Southern California Edison (SCE) tram system, in the Rush Creek drainage, was built in 1915. Carts on the tram line serviced the dams and hydroelectric power plants at Agnew and Gem lakes.

In View So many lakes. Horsetail Falls, Mount Ritter, and Banner Peak.

TRAIL BETA

- Before you're 5 miles in, just after a small unnamed lake, don't miss the left turn toward Agnew Pass.

- Garnet Lake is never signposted from this direction.

- There seem to be a thousand tracks and trails to get to Thousand Island Lake. It makes navigation a bit tricky, but also provides options for cutting the run shorter. One option is to make it a 12-mile Gem Lake loop connecting trails near Clark Lake and skipping the second half of the figure-eight.

- The unmarked cutoff trail to Garnet Lake takes attention to find and to follow.

- With so much water, avoid peak mosquito season.

Heading for higher ground on the Rush Creek Trail, with Silver Lake below.

TUOLUMNE
AND NORTH

CLOUDS REST

CLOUDS REST

TUOLUMNE

DISTANCE:

←——————→

12-mile out-and-back

GAIN:

2940 feet

DIFFICULTY:

●●○○○

HIGH POINT: 9931 ft Clouds Rest

LOW POINT: 8180 ft Sunrise Lakes Trailhead

PROFILE:

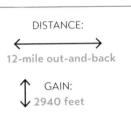

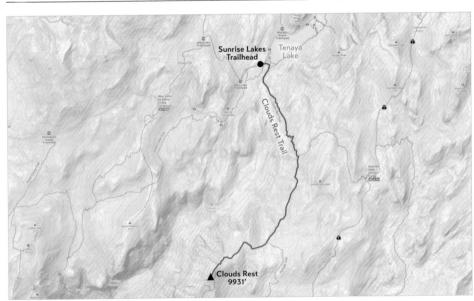

OBJECTIVE: Peak
RUNNING: 60%
MODE: Cruiser, Technical
SEASON: June–October
PERMIT: Yes, Yosemite National Park Day Entrance

ACCESS: Sunrise Lakes TH
37°49'34.0"N
119°28'11.4"W
Pit toilets

APPROACH: The trailhead is on Tioga Road within Yosemite National Park. Park at the west end of Tenaya Lake.

THE ROUTE

From Sunrise to Clouds Rest, this run is on the long end of a quick out-and-back. A steep start up rocky forest trail leads to a smooth ramp with stellar views. You probably won't be alone enjoying the view of Half Dome, Mount Watkins, and Cathedral Peak, since it's a popular day hike, and well traveled for good reason. Straightforward and easy to navigate, the run up to Clouds Rest gives you a different perspective on major Yosemite landforms.

TRAIL BETA

Sunrise or sunset are great times to be at the viewpoint if you're willing to do one direction in the dark.

MOUNT DANA & GIBBS

MOUNT DANA & GIBBS

TUOLUMNE

DISTANCE:

12.5-mile loop, clockwise

 GAIN:
4750 feet

DIFFICULTY:

HIGH POINT: **13,061 ft** Mount Dana
LOW POINT: **9700 ft** Mono Pass Trailhead

PROFILE:

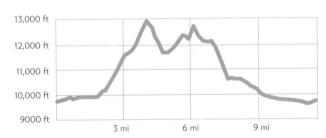

OBJECTIVE: Two Peaks
RUNNING: 50%
MODE: Steep, Technical, Adventure
SEASON: July–October
PERMIT: Yes, Yosemite National Park Day Entrance

ACCESS: Mono Pass Trailhead
37°53'28.1"N 119°15'45.2"W
Pit toilet at the parking

APPROACH: From the east, take Tioga Pass Road to the Yosemite Park entrance. The Mono Pass Trailhead Parking lot is a mile and a half inside the park.

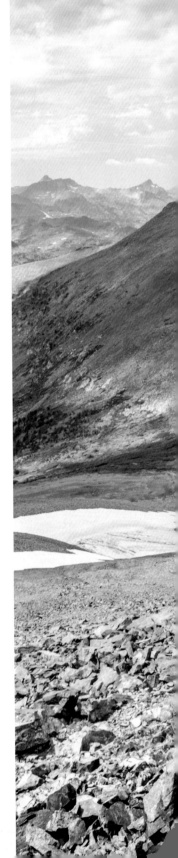

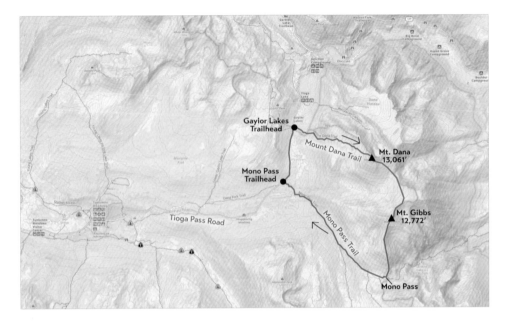

THE ROUTE

This run has a little bit of everything. Steep and rocky, soft and flowy — and how'd that mile of smooth asphalt end up in this book? The short stretch of road running is going to throw off your splits, but don't worry, the trudge up to Dana and the crumbly connector to Gibbs will slow your Strava pace back to wondering if you can even call this a run.

- First up, Dana. From the Mono Pass Trailhead, get the paved part over with, keeping eyes peeled for rubbernecking drivers as you speed back to Yosemite's Tioga entry kiosk. Jump on the Mount Dana Trail, heading east through a cluster of small lakes, and soon you'll be making your way up past treeline on a well-trodden path. Be ready for company on the way to the summit of Dana. At 13,061 feet it's the second highest in the park, famous for its views of Mono Lake.

- Beyond Dana, you'll likely see fewer folks. Moving cross-country, you're generally following the Yosemite National Park-Ansel Adams Wilderness border. The descent to the wide connecting saddle is loose, rocky terrain. Then a gentle climb leads to fun ridge scrambling to the summit of Mount Gibbs (12,779 feet).

- Take a pause on this less-frequented summit to look for Tuolumne's famous landmarks and the Kuna Crest.

- Next — you guessed it — there's more talus-hopping for a good 1.5 miles along the broad south ridge to drop you down to Mono Pass. Here you'll rejoin trail, and rejoice.

- From the pass, it's pretty meadows, woods, and beautiful, winding trail glee all the way back to the car. Yes, glee is what you'll feel, finally covering some distance, striding along a smooth, slightly downhill trail for a fast 4 miles to close the loop after so much lumbering over talus.

The Draw Tuolumne! And two of Yosemite's highest summits with views of the high country and Mono Lake.

Don't Miss After the run, don't miss the Tioga Pass Mo Mart. This Mobile gas station is famous for its better-than-gas-station food, and, if you time it right, live music. That's right, we just recommended gas-station dining.

Something Extra While you're in the area, try the often overlooked but worthwhile Gaylor Lakes Trail, a 3-mile round trip that climbs up and over the ridge west of Tioga Road. There are great views across to Dana and Gibbs.

Road to Broken Dreams Tioga Road (SR 120) is California's highest highway pass. Sierra passes have been routes for indigenous people dating back to 2000 BCE and long before that for migrating wildlife. Originally, Mono Pass was more traveled, but in 1883, misplaced mining hopes and a whole lot of labor and funds made Tioga Pass the established road. After winter closure, snow removal from Tioga Road takes 1-2 months each spring.

In View Mono Lake, Cathedral Peak, Kuna Crest, Mount Lyell, Mount Wood, Tuolumne Meadows.

TRAIL BETA

- To avoid the sometimes long lines of park entry, be sure to get to the kiosk early. That's a good idea anyway, because an early start will be more likely to get you through the loop before any summer thunderstorms.

- From Dana to Mono Pass it's all off-trail. Pick the best line over the loose terrain from Dana, working your way southeast down to the wide saddle. Start your climb to Gibbs up an open slope to the ridge. From the summit, follow the talus-y ridge south down to Mono Pass.

- Take enough water to last you through most of the loop — you won't get a refill until you top off at the lakes near Mono Pass or at a little creek on the homestretch.

- **GEAR:** Gaiters.

Kim Strom focused on the summit of Mount Gibbs.

MOUNT CONNESS

MOUNT CONNESS

TUOLUMNE

DISTANCE:

20-mile lollipop, counterclockwise

GAIN:
5450 feet

DIFFICULTY:

HIGH POINT: 12,590 ft Mount Conness
LOW POINT: 8601 ft Glen Aulin Trailhead

PROFILE:

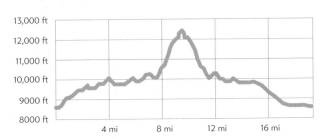

OBJECTIVE: Peak
RUNNING: 80%
MODE: Cruiser, Exposed
SEASON: June–October
PERMIT: Yes, Yosemite National Park Day Entrance

ACCESS: Glen Aulin Trailhead
   37°52′43.7″N 119°21′29.7″W
   Pit toilets at the Lembert Dome Picnic Area

APPROACH: From the east, take Tioga Pass Road to the Yosemite Park entrance. Seven miles inside the park, turn right at the Lembert Dome Picnic Area and continue to the parking along Yosemite National Park Road.

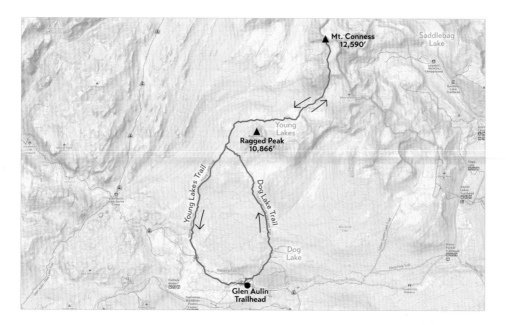

THE ROUTE

Conness is the *What's that!?* peak of Tuolumne Meadows. Seen in the distance, the massive south face of Mount Conness calls out to climbers, but runners have their own line, a flowing trail all the way from meadow to summit for a classic peak-bagging mission.

- Follow the trail for Stable Access to connect with the Dog Lake Trail. This leads to Young Lakes Trail via Dog Lake. Moving through the forest, crossing streams, opening into stretches of flat meadows and lakes, you are almost always running. After a short descent, the trail wraps around the base of Ragged Peak and arrives at Young Lakes.

- Just after Upper Young Lake, the trail begins to climb into the alpine on an improbable-looking hillside. From here, the impressive Mount Conness now seems a much smaller bump as you approach it on the firm DG trail.

- Beyond the plateau it's a blocky scramble to the top along the east ridge. Class 2. From the summit, you can see the sweeping spine of the north ridge and down onto Saddlebag Lakes.

- Retrace your scramble down to the plateau and enjoy the same DG trail that, in descent, allows for fast, carefree speeds.

- Out of the alpine and back into the trees, you're still following the same line down until 2.5 miles past Young Lakes. Take the split toward Soda Springs for the final 7 miles — all fast forest running — back to the trailhead.

The Draw Quality running to an impressive peak with an easy scramble.

Don't Miss Soda Springs: there's nothing more exciting than bubble water.

Something Extra After the run, grab your dinner stashed in the bear box and pull up a picnic table beneath Lembert Dome.

Local Lore The first known ascent of Mount Conness via the north ridge was made by one of the author's parents. Herbert Rickert and Susanne Pestel climbed the ridge in 1968. Since Hjördis' parents never felt a need to claim the first, and figured it must have been done before they did it, the FA is in many places attributed to Galen Rowell, who also found no previous record when he climbed the ridge a year later in 1969.

Climb Come back for technical rock routes on the north ridge and southwest wall.

In View Half Dome, Cathedral Range, Tenaya Lake, Saddlebag Lakes, Matterhorn Peak, Mount Dana, Ritter and Banner, Matthes Crest.

TRAIL BETA

- This is a pretty straightforward route. Just be sure to take the Young Lakes Trail via Dog Lake up, and Young Lakes Trail that passes Soda Springs down.

- **GEAR:** Mosquito repellent, gaiters.

Classic Tuolumne views full of domes and towers.

SUMMIT LAKE

SUMMIT LAKE

BRIDGEPORT

DISTANCE:

16.5-mile lollipop, counterclockwise

GAIN:
3960 feet

DIFFICULTY:

HIGH POINT: 10,480 ft Virginia Pass
LOW POINT: 8020 ft Green Creek Trailhead

PROFILE:

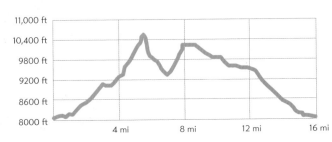

OBJECTIVE: Pass
RUNNING: 80%
MODE: Cruiser, Technical
SEASON: June–October
PERMIT: No

ACCESS: Green Creek Trailhead
   38°06′44.0″N 119°16′31.0″W
   Pit toilet, campground

APPROACH: From Highway 395, 4 miles south of Bridgeport, turn west onto Green Creek Road. Drive 11 miles on the dirt road to the trailhead.

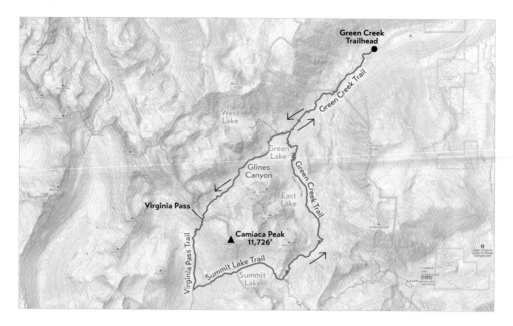

THE ROUTE

This is one of those lesser-known areas of a place we think we know well. From a backwoods launching point in the Hoover Wilderness, up two passes with surprising views into Yosemite, and mile after mile of lakeside cruising, relatively few people seem to know this area exists. It offers a day that starts with, *Where are we?* and ends with, *When do we go back?*

- Starting up the fast-flowing Green Creek Trail, easy miles and elevation fly by without noticing. If this run was out your backdoor, you'd know every rock, tree, and turn from happy repeats.

- After the first 3 miles, take the fork right briefly on the West Lake Trail before branching down a use-trail toward Green Lake. Here you're following the shore on a fainter use-trail, and starting the climb up Glines Canyon toward Virginia Pass.

- From the pass you can see all the way to Tuolumne Meadows, with surprise views of landmarks like Cathedral Peak and Half Dome. Wind your way down to the meadowed valley on the Virginia Pass Trail and into the trees until you reach the sharp turn onto the Summit Lake Trail to Summit Pass and Lake.

- From Summit Lake, you're beginning to round out the loop. When you meet the Green Creek Trail, split left toward Hoover Lake. The return winds over talus fields, through the trees, and along a line-up of smaller lakes. East Lake is the last and biggest before you drop through the woods toward Green Lake and merge back onto familiar ground.

- If you thought starting up was good, those 3 miles are even better gliding back down.

The Draw Cruiser running in a lesser-known part of the Sierra with a sneak peek into Yosemite.

Don't Miss Bodie ghost town. Less than an hour away, and in the middle of nowhere, this is one of the most famous sites of the gold rush era. The ghost town of more than 200 wooden buildings remains from a boom of nearly 10,000 people in its heyday from 1877 to 1882. More than $35 million worth of gold and silver were extracted here. The buildings still standing are kept in "arrested decay" with their contents left and preserved in place.

Very Superstitious If you visit Bodie, resist the temptation to walk off with a souvenir. Local lore has it that people who've tried to pocket objects from the ghost town were struck by a spooky string of misfortunes.

Something Extra If you're driving south you'll have a spectacular view over Mono Lake. It's definitely worth stopping along the shore to visit the moon-like landscape, tufas, brine shrimp, and California gulls. Especially beautiful at sunset and sunrise.

Wild West Rodeo Time your run on either side of the 4th of July festivities and rodeo in the old town of Bridgeport. Kick-start your hydration at the watermelon-eating contest, or try your hand at arm wrestling while your legs recover from the run.

In View Virginia Peak, Half Dome, Eichorn Pinnacle, Cathedral Peak, Mount Conness.

TRAIL BETA

- After Green Lake, look for blazes on trees to help navigate to the open meadow below Virginia Pass. Otherwise the trail is straightforward to follow.

Oranges and reds at Green Lake.

WHITE MOUNTAINS

FLYNNS

FLYNNS

WHITE MOUNTAINS

DISTANCE:

11-mile loop, counterclockwise

 GAIN:
4090 feet

DIFFICULTY:

HIGH POINT: **7055 ft**
LOW POINT: **4130 ft**

PROFILE:

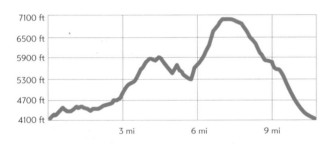

OBJECTIVE: Running
RUNNING: 75%
MODE: Cruiser, Steep
SEASON: Year round
PERMIT: No

ACCESS: Poleta 37°22'59.3"N 118°18'46.8"W
No facilities

APPROACH: From Bishop, take E Line Street, which becomes Poleta Road. After 4.5 miles, turn left onto an unnamed road. A few hundred yards further, make a hard left through a gate and follow the dirt road along the canal ditch for 1.5 miles to a cattle guard and a pullout on the right.

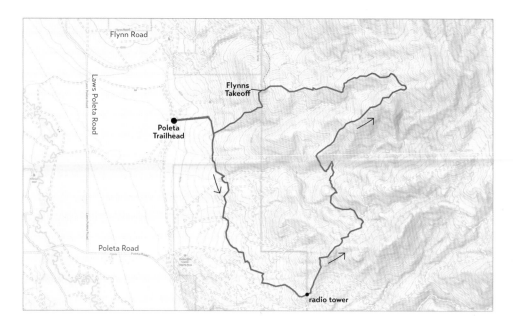

THE ROUTE

Once you've discovered the White Mountains for winter training, you'll find they offer a trove of rugged exploration and fantastic views of the valley and Sierra Crest. This tight, no-nonsense loop captures the area's wild feeling and delivers rip-roaring serpents of singletrack and efficient vert. Many of these trails, like it or not, were crafted at the wheels of dirt bikes, forcing steep lines and wild, plummeting descents. The Flynns rollercoaster.

- Head due east along the fence-lined dirt road to the base of the Whites. The track then veers south, along the mountains. Most of the way you'll be following a route signed with "R1" markers toward a landmark radio tower. You'll be happy you had the social-friendly warm-up when you hit the steep quarter mile to the tower.

- Beyond the tower, you're still covering some steep switchback-less vert.

- About a third of the way through the miles and elevation gain, the rollercoaster curves begin along singletrack that winds in and out of the canyons.

- After about 6 miles, the track briefly follows a sharper drainage southwest before the final, sweaty-even-in-winter, climb begins: 1770 feet over 1.5 miles, refreshingly steep in the land of mule-grade switchbacks.

- From a little saddle at 7000 feet, where the first piñons appear, head northwest on singletrack across a shallow drainage, then straight down the ridge to the Flynns takeoff site for paragliders. On the south side of this large clearing, where it's marked for foot traffic only, drop down the increasingly, then quad-shockingly, steep trail. Where you meet the dirt road, turn right, recognizing the short repetition back to where you parked.

High and dry at the Poleta winter playground just minutes from Bishop.

The Draw Rolling singletrack with great views of the Owens Valley and Sierra. A quick way to get some vert and a rugged mountain fix.

Don't Miss Stargazing. Looking northeast from the KUNR radio tower you'll see a cluster of geodesic domes. This is the Eastern Sierra Observatory that boasts a huge Meade Telescope and offers lecture nights and overnight stays.

Something Extra Mount Dan. At the saddle 8 miles in, instead of heading down, continue upward for another 1400 feet to gain the peaklet.

In View Sierra skyline, Owens Valley.

LADWP During the approach you'll drive across the Owens River, a reminder of the precious nature of water in this arid landscape. The Los Angeles Department of Water and Power manages the flow of water in the river system. Virtually every drop of this limited resource, originating in the snows of the Sierra, is in their hands. Acquisition of water rights in the Owens Valley has a sordid history, beginning with the underhanded methods used by William Mulholland at the turn of the century in securing land ownership and rights to the valley's water. To this day, most of the area's water is diverted to the city of Los Angeles. One of the sole bright sides of this arrangement is a hard limit on expansion and development.

TRAIL BETA

- No water — bring all you need. The foothills of the Whites can feel hot even in the winter.

Winter training with an eye on the Sierra summer objectives.

POLETA CANYON

POLETA CANYON

WHITE MOUNTAINS

DISTANCE:

12-mile loop, clockwise

GAIN:
4370 feet

DIFFICULTY:

HIGH POINT: **8814 ft**

LOW POINT: **5125 ft**

PROFILE:

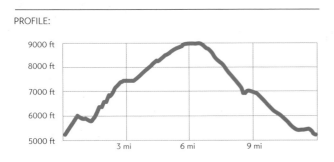

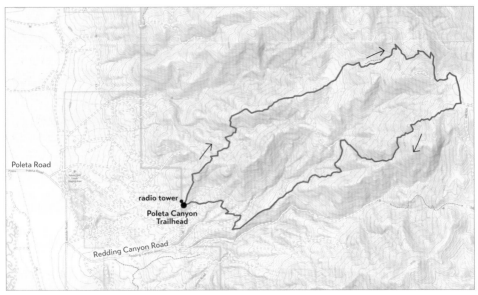

OBJECTIVE: Running
RUNNING: 75%
MODE: Cruiser, Steep
SEASON: Year round
PERMIT: No

ACCESS: Poleta
 37°21'18.5"N
 118°17'06.8"W
 No facilities

APPROACH: From Bishop, take E Line Street, which becomes Poleta Road. Turn east onto Redding Canyon Road, and after 1 mile, split left to follow the dirt road up to the radio tower.

THE ROUTE

Right out Bishop's back door, this White Mountains run climbs into sparse ancient forests with views across the Owens Valley and beyond to the classic Bishop skyline. Put this one on repeat for satisfying singletrack and winter training. Positioned beside the Flynns route, page 249, this run is simply one more example of the intricate web of use-trails in the foothills of the Whites, all of which are worth getting to know.

TRAIL BETA

With no shortage of intersecting use-trails, the route track is helpful here.

WHITE MOUNTAIN

WHITE MOUNTAIN

WHITE MOUNTAINS

DISTANCE:

←——————→

15.5-mile out-and-back

↑ GAIN:
↓ **3590 feet**

DIFFICULTY:
●●●○○

HIGH POINT: **14,252 ft White Mountain**

LOW POINT: **11,580 ft White Mountain Peak /**
Barcroft Trailhead

PROFILE:

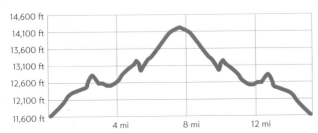

OBJECTIVE: Peak
RUNNING: 75%
MODE: Cruiser
SEASON: June–October
PERMIT: No

ACCESS: White Mountain Peak / Barcroft Trailhead
37°33'28.1"N 118°14'09.4"W
Pit toilet

APPROACH: From Highway 168, head north onto White
Mountain Road. The pavement ends at the Ancient
Bristlecone Pine Forest Visitor Center. From there it's a
slow, bumpy 16 miles.

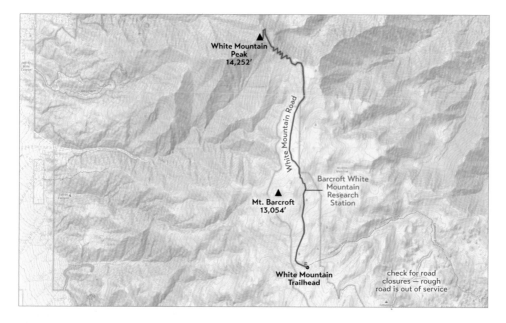

White Mountain Peak 14,252'

White Mountain Road

Barcroft White Mountain Research Station

Mt. Barcroft 13,054'

White Mountain Trailhead

check for road closures — rough road is out of service

THE ROUTE

It's not that steep or long, so why does this one feel like a hard run? You can blame it all on the altitude. Starting at nearly 12,000 feet and rolling on up to California's third highest summit, you'll be tempted to speed along the low-angle 4x4 track. Go ahead. Unless you're acclimated, see how long you last going any faster than a low-gear jog.

- Once you've made it to the trailhead, you've covered the bulk of the gain between valley and summit. It's a long drive no matter where you're coming from. Finally in your running shoes, pass by the locked gate, continuing up White Mountain Road. You'll pass through the Barcroft Station (12,470 feet), and just after it, the observatory dome on the Barcroft Plateau.

- Turn-by-turn directions to the summit are pretty simple: follow the well-worn track up to the top.

- The road is a narrow stretch of Inyo National Forest surrounded by the White Mountains Wilderness Area, which angles far down to the flats

on either side of the range. While the White Mountains might have looked like brown hills from below, up close you're traveling through a colorful, Icelandic-like landscape. Striped stretches of white, gold, gray, rust, and even green with mounds of black rock.

- The route gets gradually steeper in its final switchbacks to White Mountain Peak. On top sits the summit laboratory, and maybe a few mountain bikers bagging California's easiest 14er.

- Back down the way you came up, but breathing a little easier.

Life at high elevation for a day: running, headaches, and summit smiles.

The Draw Altitude training. Technically one of the easiest runs in this guidebook, but the altitude and the long approach make it harder.

Don't Miss The White Mountains are home to the long-living bristlecone pines (*Pinus longaeva*). The oldest one here is called Methuselah and has been rooted in thisl forest for more than 4850 years. To protect the tree, its location within the Ancient Bristlecone Pine Forest is kept secret.

Something Extra Stop at the Ancient Bristlecone Pine Forest Visitor Center for a shake-out. The Methuselah Trail is a 4.5-mile loop with 750 feet of gain. At 10,000 feet, it's a good way to start acclimating for White Mountain, or an oxygen overload afterward. Either way, you've made the drive up, so why not make a tour through these gnarly trees.

Science Mountain The White Mountain Research Center provides a base for teaching and research in physiology, astrophysics, archaeology, anthropology, ecology, biology, geology, geography, and medicine. The Barcroft Station, one of the WMRC field stations, studies the physiological effects of altitude, and was a site used by Nobel Laureate George Smoot for research in cosmic background radiation. The faint "relic radiation" provides data on the early universe. From 14 billion years ago, it's even older than those ancient bristlecones.

Local Lore Want to know more about the White Mountain Research Center? Watch the Emmy-winning documentary, *In the Shadow of White Mountain*.

In View Sierra skyline, Mount Barcroft, McAfee Meadow, Owens Valley.

TRAIL BETA

- Think about camping at the trailhead. First-come basis and free. Between the hours driving and hours running, it adds up to a long day.

- Check for road closures in the White Mountains before heading up.

- No water on route or at trailhead. Carry all you need.

- Warm layer. Even in the summer heat, there is often cold weather up top.

- GEAR: Spare tire. Seriously. The road up is rough and out of service range.

BOUNDARY PEAK

BOUNDARY PEAK

WHITE MOUNTAINS, NEVADA

DISTANCE:

←——————→

9.5-mile out-and-back

GAIN:
4060 feet

DIFFICULTY:
●●○○○

HIGH POINT: **13,140 ft Boundary Peak**
LOW POINT: **9800 ft Queen Canyon Trailhead**

PROFILE:

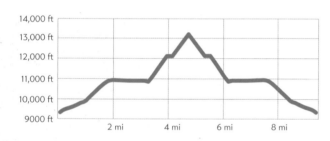

OBJECTIVE: Peak
RUNNING: 50%
MODE: Cruiser, Steep Technical
SEASON: June–October typically
PERMIT: No

ACCESS: Queen Canyon Trailhead
37°52'54.8"N 118°18'53.0"W
No facilities

APPROACH: From Highway 6, just 2.5 miles north of the California/Nevada border, take Queen Canyon Road for 6 miles. 2WD autos should park at the flat area by the Queen Mine. High-clearance 4x4 can make it to the saddle.

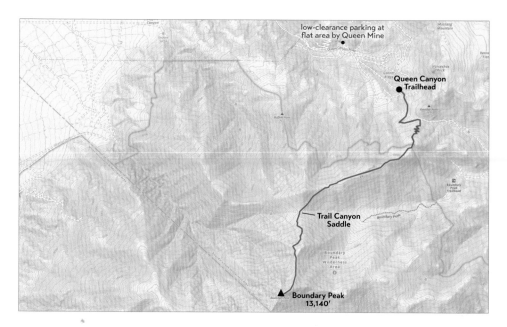

THE ROUTE

Anywhere in the Owens Valley you tend to look toward the Sierra. They're big, jagged, and demand attention. But if you turn your back on them for just a second, you'll see a whole other range running parallel. Compared to their Sierra neighbors, the White Mountains are less pointed, but their gentle curves are deceptive. From valley to peak, there's 9000 feet of relief. This run doesn't gain that much, but it's a great route for an uphill grind to a high-desert summit, the highest point in Nevada.

- Poking up right beside the CA-NV boundary line, Boundary Peak is among the abundant 13ers of the White Mountains and marks the north end of the range.

- From the Queen Canyon Trailhead, you'll need low gear to get started, either on foot or by 4x4. Continue up the rocky road, about a mile to the saddle. The trail rises from the saddle in steep switchbacks and levels out for a rolling traverse right around 10,800 feet.

- Going along, you're staring ahead at the demoralizingly distant Boundary Peak, but before you know it, you're at Trail Canyon Saddle, a flat expanse that allows a quick break to ready your legs for an imposing climb.

- Starting up the steep stuff is standard enough, but you should be comfortable moving in typical high-mountain terrain to navigate the funky final talus on the summit ridge. The enormous pile of rocks you clamber over shifts between tan and gold, and the patches of dry gray scrub lower down now look lush as they blend into a greenish hillside. Once the trail merges onto the ridge, stay on the spine when there isn't an obvious worn trail, and pick your way over boulders to the summit. Class 2-3.

- From Boundary, turn around and enjoy reversing the route back to where you started. Ridgeline to rolling to a final drop — and the long drive out.

The Draw Remote and vast. The view of the entire Sierra spread across the valley isn't so shabby.

All the Pretty Horses Wild horses might be grazing on the scrubby slopes.

Something Extra Want more of the same? From Boundary Peak, continue down the ridge and scramble up to Montgomery Peak (13,447 feet), the next summit south. It only adds 1.5 miles and 500 feet of gain, but it'll be slow going.

White Mountain Traverse From Boundary Peak, you can trace the line of the White Mountain Traverse that connects the Queen Canyon and Barcroft trailheads. The roughly 35-mile traverse is an off-trail route that scrambles along the ridge of the White Mountains, topping out at 14,252 feet on White Mountain. But that's a much longer day that would involve some logistics, like the mother of all car shuttles.

TRAIL BETA

- Even if it's a typical toasty day, there can be cold temps and an even colder wind up high.

- Bring enough water. There's no water at the trailhead or along the route. Don't even hope to find shade, either.

- GEAR: Poles and gaiters aren't bad to have as you start up from Trail Canyon Saddle.

High and very, very wild near the summit of Boundary Peak.

DEATH VALLEY

TELESCOPE PEAK

TELESCOPE PEAK

DEATH VALLEY

DISTANCE:

14-mile out-and-back

GAIN:
3280 feet

DIFFICULTY:

●●○○○○

HIGH POINT: 11,049 ft Telescope Peak
LOW POINT: 8133 ft Mahogany Flat

PROFILE:

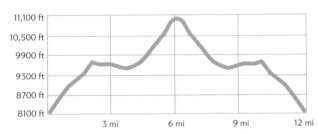

OBJECTIVE: Peak
RUNNING: 90%
MODE: Cruiser
SEASON: Year round / check road closures
PERMIT: No

ACCESS: Mahogany Flat Campground
36°13'47.5"N 117°04'06.0"W
Pit toilet at campground

APPROACH: Take Hwy 190 to Death Valley National Park. Turn onto Emigrant Canyon Road, which winds for about 30 minutes and merges into Charcoal Kiln Road. If you don't have high clearance, park at the Charcoal Kilns and run the final 1.5 miles up the road to the trailhead.

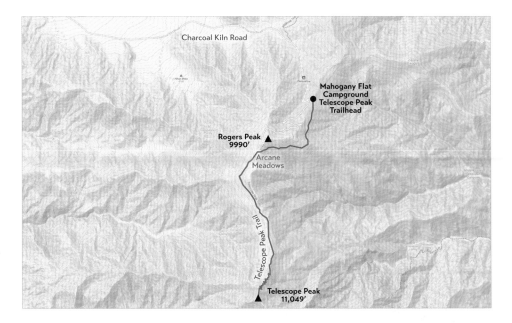

THE ROUTE

Trails don't get much better than this for running. Smooth, playfully curvy, just the right amount of steepness to move quickly uphill and charge downhill. But, there is a BUT. The area is beyond hot in summer, even high up, and arctic cold in winter. Crazily enough, this run in Death Valley is the only run we've ever started double puffed (wearing two layers of puffy jackets). It's running so good you'll forget you're in one of the world's most inhospitable landscapes.

- You really can't make a wrong turn on this one. Stay on Telescope Peak Trail. Start by angling up along the east-facing slope through a sparse forest of fresh-smelling piñons and mountain mahogany.

- Reaching Arcane Meadows, the trail passes between Rogers Peak (with radio towers) and Bennett Peak. Wrapping around Bennett Peak, the trail levels for 2 fast, flat miles, then begins its gradual climb again — this time through limber and bristlecone pines.

- A quick batch of switchbacks reminds you that you are at higher elevation. With the sudden shift to just a little bit steeper, you'll finish the climb to the summit ramp breathless. The view scans an enormous distance: from desolate Death Valley below, all the way out to the full line of Eastern Sierra summits.

- It's an out-and-back, so back down you go. Smooth, fast, and fun for an easy return.

Telescope Peak has a surprise around every turn, all good.

The Draw Easy running, harsh environment.

Don't Miss Tallest point in Death Valley. The highest/hottest/longest/biggest/most of any area is always a bit of a magnet.

Shorty's Well A tougher ascent of Telescope Peak starts at Shorty's Well (-200 feet) in Badwater Basin and winds through the south fork of Hanaupah Canyon. The 30-mile out-and-back gains 11,240 feet. That much vert makes it one of the greatest gains possible on a single peak in the contiguous US, second only to Mount Rainier.

Local Lore Telescope Peak got its name because you can see so far in every direction.

Highs and Lows In the Panamint Range, you are looking out to the highest point in the Lower 48, Mount Whitney (14,505 feet) in the distance, and down at the lowest, Badwater Basin (-282 feet).

More Highs and Lows Death Valley below holds a record temperature of 134F and a low of 15F. Dress accordingly.

In View Badwater Basin, Eastern Sierra.

TRAIL BETA

- Mahogany Flat Campground is first-come basis and free.

- In winter, December-March, the road between the Wildrose Charcoal Kilns and Mahogany Flat is often closed, closing the campground as well. Add 3 miles to your trip by parking at the kilns.

- GEAR: Bring water. There is NO water. Not at the campground or on the route. The constant exposure to sun or wind adds to your dehydration. Even the view makes you thirsty.

The trail to Telescope Peak is nearly 100% running.

WILDROSE PEAK

WILDROSE PEAK

DEATH VALLEY

DISTANCE:

8.5-mile out-and-back

GAIN:
2200 feet

DIFFICULTY:
●●○○○

HIGH POINT: 9064 ft Wildrose Peak

LOW POINT: 6875 ft Wildrose Peak TH

PROFILE:

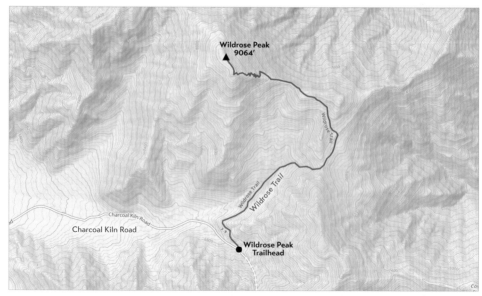

OBJECTIVE: Peak
RUNNING: 80%
MODE: Cruiser
SEASON: Year round
PERMIT: No

ACCESS: Wildrose Peak TH
36°14'48.3"N
117°04'35.0"W
Pit toilet

APPROACH: Take Hwy 190 to Death Valley NP. Turn onto Emigrant Canyon Road, which winds for about 30 minutes and becomes Charcoal Kiln Road. Parking is across from the Charcoal Kilns.

THE ROUTE

After the long approach to the trailhead, you're at the top of Wildrose Peak in a short 4 miles, having gained 2200 feet. The trail, starting beside the Wildrose Charcoal Kilns (you can't miss them), is mostly smooth through the shelter of piñons and juniper, opening up to big-vista views over Death Valley. You've got plenty of time to look around on the upper portion of the trail, where the switchbacks turn tightly enough to make you dizzy coming back down. As on Telescope Peak, you can see from the lowest to the highest point in the Lower 48.

TRAIL BETA

Take advantage of being so far away from everything and camp at one of the nearby campgrounds, then run Telescope Peak, too (page 279). Both runs can be cold and windy in the winter, and there is no water. Come prepared.

ZABRISKIE POINT

ZABRISKIE POINT

DEATH VALLEY

DISTANCE:

10-mile loop, counterclockwise

GAIN:
1920 feet

DIFFICULTY:

HIGH POINT: 900 ft

LOW POINT: -138 ft Golden Canyon TH

PROFILE:

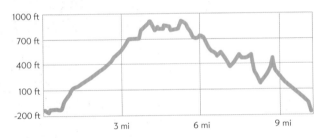

OBJECTIVE: Change of Scenery
RUNNING: 90%
MODE: Cruiser, Steep, Adventure, Exposed
SEASON: Year round
PERMIT: Death Valley National Park Entrance Fee

ACCESS: Golden Canyon Trailhead
   36°25'14.5"N 116°50'48.4"W
   Pit toilet

APPROACH: Take Hwy 190 to Death Valley National Park. Just after Furnace Creek, turn right onto Badwater Road. Parking is 2 miles down the road on the left.

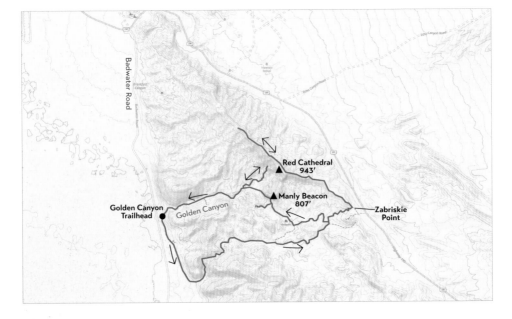

THE ROUTE

This loop is all about touristing a Death Valley attraction while running. And the running itself is otherworldly. With three out-and-backs, and plenty more canyon spokes to explore, choose to follow any number of side trips from the main loop. Visit all the sites and side trails of this curious labyrinth ... different spokes for different folks.

- Take off south on the Gower Gulch Path along the base of the sculptural formation. When the trail wraps around into the Gulch, follow this canyon all the way up to the Zabriskie Point Trail junction.

- Hook a right and follow the Zabriskie Point Trail to the small saddle north of the point. Roll along the balancy ridge of the Red Cathedral formation, a 3.5-mile, super-scenic out-and-back.

- Back at the saddle, drop down Zabriskie Point Trail. Keep right at both junctions on singletrack through the badlands maze. You're headed for a shoulder below the prominent Manly Beacon, the obvious tilted tower, to make a second out-and-back to a viewpoint.

- Next is the trail cut into the side of Manly, and a drop to the third dead-end (but worthwhile) spoke. This one takes you through steep and narrow walls to the base of the Red Cathedral.

- When you've finished exploring the labyrinth and are ready to find the exit, the pink sides of Golden Canyon lead all the way out.

TRAIL BETA

- Bring water. There is **NO water** and the air is extremely dry.

- Not recommended and potentially dangerous in hotter months. The National Park Service advises hiking in the coolest part of the day, 4am-7am, and avoiding later than 10am in the heat. It makes a nice t-shirt outing in winter.

The Draw A labyrinth of trails to explore.

Don't Miss Evening light or early morning. Shadows enhance the mesmerizing forms and colors of the starkly beautiful landscape.

Local Lore Zabriskie Point is named for Christian Zabriskie, head of the Pacific Coast Borax Company. From the 1880s, huge teams of mules were used to haul borax from Death Valley to the nearest rail line in Mojave, 165 miles away. "20 Mule Team Borax" detergent is still sold.

Tatooine Scenes of the planet Tatooine in *Star Wars: A New Hope* and *Return of the Jedi* were filmed here in Golden Canyon and nearby locations within Death Valley.

LSD French philosopher Michel Foucault attributed the psychedelically inspired shift of his ideologies to a 1975 acid trip at Zabriskie Point.

In View Badlands, salt flats of Badwater Basin, Telescope and Wildrose peaks.

RUN RANKING BY DIFFICULTY

1 EASY

Bishop Canal	135
McMurry Meadows	93
Alabama Hills	49
Mammoth Rock	197
Tablelands	159
Tungsten Peak	139

2 MODERATE

Wildrose Peak	287
Clouds Rest	219
Lower Rock Creek	171
Tungsten Hills	143
Zabriskie Point	291
Deer Lakes Loop	189
Druids/Waganobe	127
Flynns	249
Poleta Canyon	257
Summit Lake	239
Mount Starr	163
Telescope Peak	279

3 HARD

Mount Gould	69
Mount Goode	107
Garnet Lake	209
White Mountain	261
Minarets	201
Boundary Peak	269
Mount Dana and Gibbs	223
Mount Langley	41
Mount Baldwin	181

4 VERY HARD

Mount Conness	231
Mount Whitney / Tumanguya	53
Cardinal Mountain	85
Cloudripper	97
Granite Park	151
Mount Tyndall	61

5 NAILS

Lamarck Col to Piute Pass	119
Rae Lakes	77
Evolution	115

SAGE TO SUMMIT
Q & A WITH HOWIE AND KAREN SCHWARTZ

Howie and Karen Schwartz are both enthusiastic trail runners and mountain athletes who have lived together in Bishop, California, since 2001. Howie is a UIAGM mountain guide and an owner/manager of Sierra Mountain Guides, Inc. Karen was the mayor of Bishop in 2018 and 2022, and manages their business, Sage to Summit, a mountain shop and climbing gym on Main Street.

What makes the Eastern Sierra special for trail running?

Karen: Many trails are perfect for running. The weather is fantastic, the scenery is majestic, and you can move through multiple ecosystems on a single route.

Howie: We live in the high desert at 4000 feet beneath peaks above 14,000 feet on both sides. The Owens Valley has endless world-class running terrain — no brush or boulders, no itchy plants to beware of, not much dangerous wildlife, and little precipitation. The running season is year-round, so if you don't like the weather, start lower or higher to get just what you want. Desert, forest, mountains — it's all right here.

How have you seen the sport change from when you started until today? And do you see trail running evolving in any direction?

Karen: When I first opened Sage to Summit, Marie Boyd, the founder of the Bishop High Sierra Ultramarathons, cultivated a core ultra-running community. She informally hosted a week where local runners would complete huge days in the mountains. They called it the Bishop Ball Buster. Some of the runs started at South Lake and folks would run for two hours and then turn around so everyone finished more or less at the same time. They also ran Lower Rock Creek, ate lunch at Tom's Place, and then would run back down. The Sky Marathon, from North Lake to Pine Creek, was always on their list. Marie told me that if there was a hot ditch in the area, they would

always stop for a soak. Evenings were dinners and drinks and more running the next day. The group consisted of longtime passionate ultra-runners who participated in the sport before it took off. Now that trail running is so much bigger, it is harder to organize informal running events like the Ball Buster on public lands. Too many people would participate for it to be "informal." However, the sport is so huge, people are now doing their own personal versions of the Ball Buster all the time.

In the Sierra, the sport has changed from a small core group of people to large numbers of runners. The running community is also very diverse. Many people I know have recently taken to running ultramarathons in the mountains but do not participate in organized races. Many climbers who do not consider themselves runners are also dabbling in big mountain-running days. It is such a fantastic way to spend the day in the Sierra, especially if you want to check out new terrain but have limited time. Since I opened the store in 2006, I have seen people get inspired by learning about running huge mountain loops and immediately try it themselves. If someone is already mountain fit, then it is likely that they will be hooked on mountain running.

Howie: Oh yeah, I almost forgot trail running is considered a sport! Personally, I can't risk chronic injuries that will affect my guiding, so I listen attentively to my body, try my best to temper my competitive drive, and treat running as a way of connecting myself with nature.

Local Eastern Sierra races are fun because they are very social, and the community

support for the athletes is astounding. Suffering builds strength and character that is also a luxury of extreme privilege when we can choose it. I think there are more people than ever these days who crave trail running as a test of personal endurance and for outdoor inspiration in their lives. Beyond organized events, gear, and the internet, trail running continues to be a primordial and pure pursuit.

What do trail runners come to the Sierra for and how have your businesses adapted in response?

Karen: Most of the trail runners that come to Sage to Summit are interested in either huge mountain days or multi-day fastpacking loops. Typically, they have checked out the runs on our website and have a tick list of what they want to do. Most of the questions center around nutritional needs and gear, and what type of running pack they should use.

Howie: Sage to Summit has always been a place to gear up and get information to support local trail running. Sierra Mountain Guides expanded our programs years ago to include a few classic itineraries for multi-day trail-running tours both here and internationally, but I think these have served mostly to help runners follow their own unguided inspirations, which is perfectly fine by me!

Favorite Sierra trail?

Karen: Sky Marathon with variations. I love French Canyon and it is always fantastic to do the proper route. However, veering up toward Royce Lakes and looping down through Honeymoon Lakes is a fantastic deviation. I enjoy bagging a peak and shorter mountain runs before or after work.

Howie: The best Sierra trails are where there are no trails! The kind of running I prefer has always been of the steep-mountain variety. For a more civilized trail-running experience, the High Sierra Hut-to-Hut Loop, a tour offered by Sierra Mountain Guides, gets high marks.

BISHOP LOVE

The town of Bishop is, was, or may become home to each of the authors. We'd like to give a big thanks to the community and friends who joined us on runs, shared trail tips, made dinners, fed the cat and tucked in the chickens, offered up couches, spare rooms, and all sorts of support during this process:

Julie Faber, Keith Rainville, Ali Rainville, Ian Walker, Mark Postle, Kate Rutherford, Allan Pietrasanta, Karen and Howie Schwartz, Steve Elia, Ann Camacho, Monica Prelle, Ariana Wylie, Simon and Moran Ludwig, Dani Reyes-Acosta, Jed and Diane Beebe, Amy Sturgill, Dallas Frederick, Peter Schultz, Shauna Murray, Finn Zeugswetter, Kris Hohag, Jenica Law, Andy Patterson, Clare Gallagher, Krissy Moehl, Scott Johnston — if we forgot anyone, we owe you a beer.

We want to offer a special thank-you to Julie Faber for keeping our bodies up and running in the backyard and in the backcountry.

Backcountry bodywork by Julie Faber.

THE AUTHORS

Dan Patitucci is a professional mountain-sport photographer and athlete with more than 30 years experience running and climbing in the Sierra. He is married to Janine, and the couple lived in Bishop for nearly 10 years before moving to Switzerland. Along with Kim Strom, the pair also produced *Run the Alps Switzerland* and ALPSinsight, the trail-running guide and resource to the Swiss Alps. Dan's photography work has taken him running and climbing in mountain ranges all over the world, from the Himalaya to Iceland to Patagonia, and all throughout Europe. He still calls the Sierra "home."

Originally from Switzerland, Janine Patitucci is a professional mountain-sport photographer and digital-imaging specialist at PatitucciPhoto. As a lover of maps and geography, Janine masterminded many of the runs in this guidebook, as well as the runs in the team's Swiss Alps guidebook, *Run the Alps Switzerland*, and the Alps' Via Valais multi-day trail-running tour.

From climbing 8000-meter peaks and Patagonian spires to working as a rock and alpine guide in the Sierra, Hjördis Rickert has a broad, lifelong mountain background. A Bishop local, she's traveled and photographed in mountain ranges all over the world, and has recently discovered the freedom of running through her home range with a much lighter pack.

Kim Strom is a mountain runner and cancer survivor. Since 2016, she has worked with PatitucciPhoto as a writer, photographer, and athlete. She co-founded both Elevation: The Alps Trail & Peak Running Resource and the Via Valais, and co-authored the *Run the Alps Switzerland* guidebook. Her feature stories have appeared in Patagonia's *The Cleanest Line*, *Runner's World*, and *Trail Runner*, as well as numerous outdoor blogs and other publications.

OUR FAVORITE RUNS
Dan: Cloudripper and Mount Tyndall
Janine: Mount Langley and Mount Baldwin
Hjördis: Flynns and Cardinal Peak
Kim: Granite Park and Tungsten Peak

I
Am
Nuumu
Ancestors
Live through me
Tsawu naamati nuu
I feel good
When i run
Among the mountains
My spirit is renewed

My body strengthened
Mind clear
No fear
Focused
Running is good medicine
Physical. Mental.
Spiritual
Primal
Here
I am
Io
Nu

— Kris Hohag